ON FOOT IN THE AFRICAN BUSH

ON FOOT IN THE AFRICAN BUSH
Adventures of Safari Guides

JEFF WILLIAMS

Whittles Publishing

Published by

Whittles Publishing Ltd,
Dunbeath,
Caithness, KW6 6EG,
Scotland, UK

www.whittlespublishing.com

© 2020 Jeff Williams

ISBN 978-184995-459-4

Front cover photograph - Brett Horley

contents

Preface vii

Acknowledgements ix

1   How it all started 1

2   The king of the beasts 12

3   Dagha boys 25

4   A place called Leeuwfontein 35

5   Rhinoceros 45

6   More elephant moments 50

7   Creatures from the deep 66

8   By moonlight 73

9   Snakes 79

10 Learning the game 88

11 Simple pleasures 95

12 More about cats 106

13 The most dangerous animal of all 113

14 Some special insights 121

15 Into the future 129

The contributors 139

Author leading a group in the Greater Kruger National Park, South Africa. *(Brett Horley)*

The Author

Jeff Williams was born to Welsh-speaking parents from Swansea though he lives in the north of Wales. His professional life has been very varied, starting as a soldier in the regular army and finishing as a hospital paediatrician. He has had five books published, all about mountaineering or walking and including *Walking in the Drakensberg* (2nd edition, 2017) and *Walking in the Ardennes* (2014). His retirement interest is anything and everything about the African bush to which he has a true addiction, developing florid symptoms if deprived of it for any length of time. He is a FGASA-registered Trails Guide and teaches Trails Guiding at Motsumi Bush Courses.

Preface

Right from my first tourist visit the African bush pulled me in like a magnet and wouldn't let go. First Botswana and South Africa, later Kenya, Tanzania and Namibia, it was all the same story. I had to go back.

As the introductory chapter relates I didn't originally set out to be a safari guide. That just sort of happened with retirement. But having achieved my qualifications, the realisation dawned on me that many guests who walk with a guide in the bush have little understanding of the scope of knowledge, experience and bush savvy required by guides to safely manage the ever-present potential for encounters with dangerous animals, sometimes at very close quarters.

The stories that were told to me by these guides, occasionally amusing, usually dramatic and not infrequently intensely harrowing, are what triggered this book. They have informed, educated and fascinated me. I very much hope that it does the same for you, the reader.

Jeff Williams
Llanfairtalhaiarn, North Wales

Acknowledgements

The acknowledgements section is a challenge for any author; almost inevitably someone doesn't get onto the page. If this applies to anyone reading this book then I offer profuse apologies for the omission.

Where to start? Top of the list must come those guides who freely gave their time writing or relating their stories directly to me, and in some cases then had to put up with my emailed queries to ensure I had transcribed the facts correctly and without too much embellishment. Some of their own photographs were terrifically helpful in setting the scene. On several occasions there was an extremely emotional re-living of the experience: one in particular brought me to tears as I listened. Without all these people there would be no book.

Books don't happen without a production team. Whittles have been a great pleasure to work with. Clever ideas for designs and styles were presented to me, prompt and courteous responses to my obsessive queries landed on my desk and, most importantly for authors, regular updates as to progress. This was especially important as it took place during the very difficult time of the SARS-CoV-2 pandemic with its attendant disruption. Thank you Keith, Kerrie and colleagues. The book was edited by Caroline Petherick. I can only say that it was a privilege to be guided by someone of her talent and her constructive commentary. Not only did I enjoy the process but I learned a lot too.

It's important that I make special mention of the principal mentors in my journey into guiding. Ian Owtram led me gently but expertly through the early stages and then Bennet de Klerk at Motsumi Bush Courses grabbed me by the scruff of the neck, encouraged me to stay the course and finally pushed me over the line to qualify as a trails guide. I am old enough to be his father. But in bush skill and experience I was his babe in arms: he watched me learning to crawl and now observes my primitive attempts at walking with tolerance and kindness. Brett Horley, during our several journeys in the bush together, was always inspirational as well as being a courteous and tolerant supervisor of my first very tentative forays as a qualified lead guide. On a couple of occasions he introduced me to guides who would 'like to walk as your back-up', a sort of covert and unspoken arrangement to give me confidence and possibly keep me out of trouble. You did it well and discreetly, Brett.

My friend Patricia Goodwin, also a lead trails guide, has been my companion on many journeys in southern Africa. She has been responsible for introducing me to several storytellers as well as taking a bundle of photographs to illustrate their tales. Pat, thank you so much for your story, for your comradeship and for 'having my back' during our adventures.

Last, but certainly not least, is my wife Maryann, herself a highly experienced safari traveller (a lot of the photographs are hers), who has tolerated (just) my many bush absences with great forbearance. She has been a good constructive critic: her major contribution has been to read and re-read the whole manuscript, making sensible suggestions about dodgy grammatical constructions, words repeated several times in a paragraph and impenetrably long sentences. Surprisingly, we haven't had too many significant 'domestics' about this, which is more a tribute to her tact than to my ready acceptance of criticism.

1 HOW IT ALL STARTED

It was noon. A sunny winter day at a game lodge in South Africa. Six guests had asked to go for a walk in the bush, and experienced walking guide Owen Booysen, assisted by another guide, was to lead them. They headed out to a nearby dam that had a reputation for great sightings, though when they got there it was a bit disappointing: the only inhabitant was an old hippo bull, sleeping peacefully and apparently uninterested in them or, indeed, anything else.

Facing down a large elephant on foot. *(Brett Horley)*

But it was a nice day, almost no breeze and not too hot, so they decided to return by a different route, which would pass the lodge waterhole. This was another place where there were excellent viewing opportunities, so they approached very carefully. The only sound to be heard was the low hum of the swimming pool pump at the lodge. There was a short slope leading down to the water, a large jackalberry tree by the water inlet and some scattered shrubs. That was enough cover for all manner of surprises. Caution had to be the watchword. Owen explained to his guests that although elephants were huge they used cover really well and sometimes you didn't see them until you were right on top of them. How prescient were those words!

Just as he uttered them he heard a noise. A blowing sound. Elephant! It appeared from behind the tree, about 15 metres away. A bull of about 25–30 years old with beautiful long tusks. The elephant saw them. Immediately he lifted his head high and spread his ears wide, which made him look much, much bigger. Quickly, Owen asked his back-up guide to move the guests a little way back behind some shrubs. They would be less visible there and maybe less of an irritant to the elephant. The elephant walked slowly towards him and Owen spoke firmly. 'Hey boy, come on now, relax. We aren't here to harm you. We just bumped into you by accident.' The response was instantaneous: a short charge. At 10 metres the elephant stopped and stared down at Owen. Given that the shoulder height of a bull may be 4 metres or more, this was very close and very daunting. The animal drew dust up with his trunk and threw it at him. Owen needed to appear relaxed. He lifted his rifle into the air to suggest more height. In response the elephant trumpeted loudly, picked up some grass with his trunk and threw it at Owen.

'Come on, boy, relax. We'll move away when you move away.' After a few seconds the elephant moved slowly away towards the drainage line at the other end of the dam. But all the time he maintained his dominating posture with his tail standing straight out – he wasn't at all relaxed. Suddenly he turned and trotted back to the same point, though at least he wasn't throwing things now. Finally he retreated once more and disappeared from sight into the tree-shrouded drainage line which fed the waterhole.

Momentary relief. Owen turned to move back slowly towards his guests but no sooner had he started when he heard branches breaking off to his left amongst the bushes that that shielded the drainage line. It was the elephant again; he hadn't given up yet. Once more Owen held his rifle high and shouted. The elephant went back into cover but instantly turned, re-emerged and charged. Yet again he stopped at about 10 metres. Owen shouted to his back-up to lead the guests quickly back towards the lodge whilst he managed the elephant. The animal repeated the withdrawal and charge sequence twice more, and each time Owen shouted loudly and banged the stock of his rifle. By now he had recognised that this was a demonstration of dominance rather than a threat to his life, though he had been correct in not making that assumption earlier. If he had panicked and run the outcome might have been very different. A few minutes later he was able to slip away to rejoin his guests at the lodge and leave the elephant, who suddenly seemed to have lost interest in the business. No-one at the lodge had seen anything of the encounter. As far as they were concerned it had been a nice, gentle after-breakfast walk!

This book is a compilation of serious encounters like this that have confronted qualified guides – some more experienced, some less – when walking in the bush. The accounts paint an honest and sometimes very vivid canvas of how fast things happen and how professional guides react under pressure, and often their subsequent analysis of the potential crisis. With three notable exceptions, two of which did not occur at the time of the event, no fatal outcomes to guides, clients or animals are recorded here. This is not a device to spare the feelings of more sensitive souls, but is a fair reflection of the very low incidence of unhappy outcomes. The stories were all written, recorded or reported to me by field guides, and in one case the wife of a guide, from southern or eastern Africa. Several of the accounts are my own. Some of them were sufficiently harrowing to rekindle long-buried emotions, and I'm particularly grateful that the people concerned were prepared to share so willingly what clearly in many cases were still painful memories.

My own journey through guide training started a long time ago. It was a hot day. September in the Okavango Delta is often hot, drying out the landscape and concentrating the animals around any available water and so, for visitors, it's a good time to be there. By 7.30 a.m. my wife Maryann and I had crossed the mirror-calm water of the lagoon adjacent to the camp in our *mokoro* (a traditional dugout canoe), an almost inaudible lapping of water against the hull the only evidence of our passage. The implied threat from the resident hippo had not materialised, and we stepped out onto the shore slightly relieved and slightly disappointed in equal measure.

Maryann crossing a lagoon in the Okavango Delta by mokoro. *(Jeff Williams)*

A sub-optimally equipped walking guide for a dangerous game area.
(*Maryann Williams*)

We weren't new to Africa and vehicle-borne safaris, but setting out on foot in the bush for the first time felt like a big moment. Our guide, David, a very slight and rather reserved local guy, led us away from the water at an easy pace carrying in one hand a large cool-box containing water, Sauvignon Blanc and peanuts, and in the other my newly purchased, almost virgin, copy of *Newman's Birds of Southern Africa*. No rifle, no radio and no briefing. It was open country with great visibility and only isolated wild fig trees lining the waterway, so, in hindsight, no danger of being surprised.

Later we passed through an area of sparse bushes and more trees, and it was here that we saw our first significant beasts. Three giraffes peered at us over the branches of some isolated acacias and immediately took flight with their typically deceptive fast, though slow-motion-looking gait. A large and unidentified olive-coloured snake bolted down a large hole at the base of a large termite mound, and from the top of the same mound several dwarf mongooses popped up to see what the excitement was about and just as quickly ducked down again. New names, new experiences; it was just magical.

Then, as is often the case, out of the blue came a touch of excitement. We had just emerged from some more dense but low bushes onto a sort of animal highway when David stopped dead in his tracks. He pointed to the right. 'Lions,' he said, without much drama – but added those immortal words: 'whatever you do, don't run'. This was the first time I'd heard the phrase and had no idea that it would be something I would repeat to others many, many times in the future. To our inexperienced eyes the male looked huge. Typically he lazily levered himself upright, glanced momentarily towards us and, seeing no immediate threat, pushed off leisurely with his three attendant females. They'd been only about 50 metres away and although we spent some time examining the tracks there was no question of any follow-up. I was hooked. Although I didn't recognise it at the time, this holiday was the prompt that tipped me over the edge into an overwhelming passion for the bush and everything to do with it. The question was, how could I develop it?

Retirement rarely hits you like a train. It creeps towards you stealthily, an assassin creeping through the mists of the future. Financial planning is common. But emotional and practical day-to-day planning tends to fall into the 'it's a long way off, there's no point in worrying about it now' category. Everyone has advice for the imminent retiree. 'Do all the things in home and garden that you never had time for'; 'spend much more time with your partner and / or grandchildren'; 'be positive, go out and do things, join a club'.

I went to Africa.

Enrolment on a guide training course was and still is straightforward. Many courses attract a multinational group, and whilst the majority are young there is a wide span of ages. I was 63. The backgrounds of the participants are varied, and I suspect that

The guilty party – *Parabuthus transvaalicus* prepares to enter author's room. (*Jeff Williams*)

my course was as typical as any. There was a lady hairdresser, a university zoology student, a farmer's son, a young Shangaan guy – already a tracker at a famous lodge – and a couple who were simply embedded in nature. Less youthful was James from the UK who was in his 50s, had sold his engineering business to start a new life in Africa, and was already working in the bush. We became, and still are, firm friends and he has contributed to this book. Finally there was me, with a military and then medical background. Truly the grandfather. This variety is typical of guides in training, though nearly all have shared a fascination and enthusiasm for nature for many years.

The first night of my six-week basic course was eventful. It started with the evening meal and the early, tentative verbal explorations that you hope will lead towards forging a great camaraderie over the weeks ahead. After the meal and a few beers it was bedtime. It was at that moment I noticed that the door to my room that opened into a central courtyard had a distinct gap underneath; a perfectly negotiable gap for any manner of small beast. I watched with horrid fascination as first a spider – the largest I'd seen in my life– and then a large scorpion scuttled through to explore my residence. This was not good. Action was required. Four of us trainee guides, now brimming over with confidence and with at least eight hours of bush experience between us, decided that all the furniture in my room together with the bedding should be removed and everything carefully inspected. Only this way could I reasonably expect to survive the night. So wardrobe, bedside table, chair and bed were carried outside, followed by a violent, arms-length shaking of the bed linen. Nothing. And the wardrobe was empty. A cursory examination of the now bare 8 square metres of concrete floor was unrevealing. This was puzzling, but everything was duly returned to its place in the room. An hour or so later I had summoned sufficient courage to slip between the sheets, but lay motionless lest the slightest movement might attract dangerous arthropods. But at 2 a.m. I awoke with the terrible realisation that snakes, too, might easily slither in, so I improved security by strategically siting a bath towel and my dressing gown to completely fill the under-door space. Safe at last, I slept until sunrise, when I heard the welcoming clink of coffee cups, the invariable precursor to the daily early morning walk in the bush.

I was distinctly wary, verging on anxious, about coping with the course content. Subjects like geology, astronomy and weather systems had hitherto been a closed book to me. Studying grasses left me cold. But taxonomy appealed to the tiny residual vestige of scientist that remained within and, as I'm a bit of a birder, I found the ornithology section fascinating. Fortunately the course instructor, Ian Owtram, was a fine teacher, a highly experienced guide and a most pleasant person, which taken all together makes a great package. But the idea of doing examinations had no appeal whatsoever. It was 35 years since I'd taken one and I had no enthusiasm about starting again. I could have just done the course and politely declined the opportunity to place myself before the examiners but I was too cowardly to opt out. In the event it went fine. The written paper was OK and the practical, with real tourists as guinea-pigs, was surprisingly more fun than stressful.

After basic guide training I had become convinced that there was something very, very special about walking in the bush. Many people would agree that it's by far and away the best way to experience the real wild Africa. The sounds and the silence, the smells, the touching of tree bark smoothed by an elephant or a rhino, the vision of a zebra stallion staring at you trying to decipher whether you intend harm towards him or his harem … there are so many things which can combine to create a state of mind that is difficult to reproduce anywhere else. In its own way it makes for an almost spiritual experience. Although for most people the important part of the joy and wonder of these forays on foot is to find and watch animals, the vast majority are easily drawn into the fascination of many other aspects of the bush, from bird identification to insect tracks, from geological features to the traditional medicinal uses of certain trees. Overall a perfect cornucopia of nature.

Most walking guides will impress on their guests that they will use their best endeavours to get close enough to animals for a good view and a decent photograph, and no closer. They will explain that it is never, ever, about seeing how close you can get. Ideally the animal shouldn't even know that you are there and, if they do, never be more than alerted to your presence. If the moment arrives when that animal is faced with a decision to run away or to fight then the guide has either been simply unlucky or incautious. However, notwithstanding the best efforts of guides, adverse incidents can and do occur, and the potential dangers of walking in a dangerous game area must never be underestimated. There are dangers, and it requires considerable knowledge, experience, common sense and focus – always focus – to best avoid trouble.

So, having achieved a basic guide qualification, how do you go about becoming a walking guide? The trite answer is that you walk in the bush. A lot. In South Africa this walking must be with an approved mentor, recording every walk and all its details in your log book. The target is 200 hours and, having successfully overcome the hurdles of the written and shooting examinations, to present yourself for assessment as a trails guide. This qualification, which in different countries may carry a different name, allows and equips you to lead parties on foot in dangerous game areas. The best way to start this process is to sign up for a course, the longer the better, during which you are coached in all the important and relevant aspects towards becoming a knowledgeable and safe pair of hands on a bush walk. After a couple of hundred hours of walking you are certainly no expert, but should be sufficiently bush savvy to provide an interesting and safe experience for guests. Understandably, having achieved this goal you can't just find an interesting-looking dangerous game area and start walking. All land of this type belongs to someone – a national park or a safari lodge for example – and you need their permission to walk there, which in practice, with rare exceptions, means being employed by them.[1]

Almost all lodges in South Africa require their walking guides to carry a rifle. There are several reasons for this. At the top of the list could be that many guests feel safer if there's a weapon in the party, and expect there to be one. In addition there

---

1 The issue of foreign nationals gaining a work permit in most southern and east African countries is beyond the scope of this book.

8   A guide on the range doing her advanced rifle handling test. *(Bob Nixon)*

It's not just about speed and accuracy. Here, guide Patricia
Goodwin makes her rifle safe before a walk. *(Jeff Williams)*

is an insurance issue – in the unlikely event that an incident occurs in the bush in
the absence of a rifle, somebody might be more likely to take legal action. On rare
occasions carrying a rifle may be life-saving. The result of this policy is that all guides
who walk in dangerous game areas have to undertake regular shooting assessments.
No pass, no walk is the rule. The training focuses on loading, shooting and reloading
very quickly at short range, 12 metres or less, and handling a firearm safely. This has a
clear argument underpinning it. If there is a life-threatening charge, then it is, with rare
exceptions, from close range, so guides should train for it. Having said all that, very few
of today's guides have ever fired their rifle in anger.

I need to be honest and admit that the first walk that I led as the only rifle-carrying
guide after qualification was fraught with anxiety – for me, at any rate. This had started
the night before, lying in a tent wondering why on earth I was putting myself through
all this stress at over 70 years of age. Loading the rifle and trying to look confident and
positive outside the lodge the following morning I found equally challenging. But after
half an hour of walking, with no sightings of anything larger than a dung beetle, I began
to relax. That was the moment we came across a very large number of elephants. More
than 50 of them in small, mobile groups. The nearest was about 100 metres away and
upwind of us, so probably hadn't yet caught our scent. My fascinating discourse on their
social structure was interrupted by the realisation that we were surrounded. Should we
stay or should we go? And if it was 'go', where to? I racked my brains. A flashback. Once

Complete a page per day as per AM (morning) and PM (Afternoon) walks.

DATE	Guiding area – Name (National Park, Private Game Reserve, etc.)	Lead Guide Name	Back-up Guide Name	Trail group size
08/11/2015				
Hours walked AM: 3.5	KLASERIE, Greater Kruger NP	Self		3
		Did you do this walk as a **Participant** on a training or mentored walk? NO		

ANIMAL INFORMATION

	Animal Species	Animal group size	Animal group structure	Distance from animals (±) m	Mentor's Signature
1	ELEPHANT	Many	Breeding Herd	40~	
2	ELEPHANT.	Many	Breeding Herd	150 m	
3					
4					
5					

DATE	Guiding area – Name (National Park, Private Game Reserve, etc.)	Lead Guide Name	Back-up Guide Name	Trail group size
__/__/____				
Hours walked PM:				
		Did you do this walk as a **Participant** on a training or mentored walk?		

ANIMAL INFORMATION

	Animal Species	Animal group size	Animal group structure	Distance from animals (±) m	Mentor's Signature
1					
2					
3					
4					

[This page and opposite] Author's logbook entry of the incident of being surrounded by elephants.

before in training our party had been surrounded by groups of elephant plus black and white rhinos.[2] The animals largely ignored us and eventually moved away. Fast forward

2 The white rhinoceros. How did it get its name?
A commonly related story goes like this. Old Dutch settlers referred to the animal as having a 'widje' lip. On hearing this, English speakers assumed that what was actually meant was 'white' and not 'wide'. Bingo, the name 'white rhinoceros' was born. Often, extra weight is added to the tale by pointing out that the beast isn't white. But the story doesn't withstand close scrutiny. Some facts:
1. The first reference to the same animal in Dutch hunting journals dates back to 1690 when it was called 'witte rhinoster'. This is the oldest 'Afrikaans' name for it.
2. The word 'wijd' (or wijde, adjective) in the Middle Dutch of the 17th century could not be used to indicate a body part and was a word used to indicate distance from one place to another. For wide in the anatomical sense, the word 'breed' or 'breede' was used.
3. In 1812, when William Burchell shot his specimens of the animal at Chué Springs, it was in an area of the Northern Cape dotted with calcrete pans. Any rhino wallowing there, as rhinos do, would appear very white. He did not give it an English name though to some it became known as Burchell's rhinoceros. Burchell allotted it a scientific name, *Rhinoceros simus*.

| Accumulated hours as Lead Guide: 13 | Accumulated hours as Back-up Guide: 89 | Accumulated hours as a Participant: 180 |

ACTIVITY SUMMARY / ENCOUNTER DESCRIPTION / INCIDENT REPORT

This page is for YOU to provide a brief description of the guided activity and locality, encounters, or if there is a need for an incident report or any further comments by the Mentor

INITIAL PLAN WAS TO TRACK ELEPHANT GROUP THAT HAD TRAVERSED THE CAMP IN THE NIGHT.

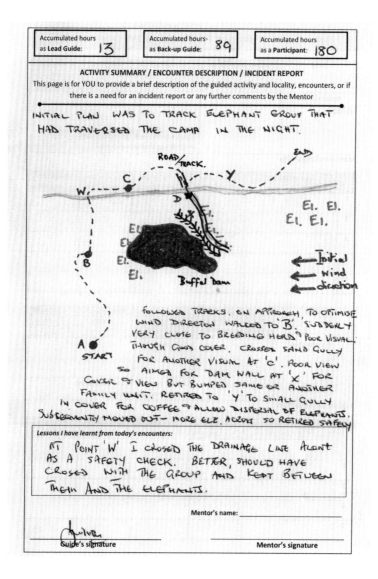

FOLLOWED TRACKS, ON APPROACH, TO OPTIMISE WIND DIRECTION WALKED TO 'B'. SUDDENLY VERY CLOSE TO BREEDING HERD? POOR VISUAL THOUGH GOOD COVER. CROSSED SAND GULLY FOR ANOTHER VISUAL AT 'C'. POOR VIEW SO AIMED FOR DAM WALL AT 'X' FOR COVER & VIEW BUT BUMPED SAME OR ANOTHER FAMILY UNIT. RETIRED TO 'Y' TO SMALL GULLY IN COVER FOR COFFEE & ALLOW DISPERSAL OF ELEPHANTS. SUBSEQUENTLY MOVED OUT— MORE ELE. ACROSS SO RETIRED SAFELY

Lessons I have learnt from today's encounters:

AT POINT 'W' I CROSSED THE DRAINAGE LINE ALONE AS A SAFETY CHECK. BETTER, SHOULD HAVE CROSSED WITH THE GROUP AND KEPT BETWEEN THEM AND THE ELEPHANTS.

Mentor's name: _____

_____
Guide's signature

_____
Mentor's signature

back to the present; we stayed put. Actually, not exactly where we were but close by, sitting in some comfortable rocks and bushes in a shallow drainage line. We drank coffee, and this, I hoped, would demonstrate my coolness under fire as well as steadying my nerves. Twenty minutes later we emerged and couldn't see an elephant anywhere. After that first walk my confidence grew. The trick is to allow this to happen gradually without ever, ever becoming overconfident. If you do, the bush will catch you out, and it may bite.

4. The famous William Cornwallis-Harris, a good wildlife artist and ruthless hunter, described the animal as 'often approaching a creamy colour'.
5. The early settlers at the Cape soon encountered black rhinoceros (then called African rhinoceros) but no other species of rhino existed there. Only much later when they strayed north would they find the 'witte rhinoster' in the Kalahari thornveld savannah, and would compare their colour (white) with the morphologically distinct and already named African rhinoceros.
So there you have it. White rhinoceros. Not truly descriptive but historically accurate.
(I am grateful to Bennet de Klerk, Director of Motsumi Guide Training School, for this discourse)

2 THE KING OF THE BEASTS

The contraction in the lion population has contributed to its already well-established position as the animal most wildlife visitors want to see, especially those who have never before seen a lion in the wild. They still attract adjectives such as 'noble', 'majestic' and 'brave', so much so that it has been suggested, slightly tongue-in-cheek, that its longstanding title of King of the Beasts has been supplanted by King of the Clichés.

Often lions can be bold and unpredictable, but on the other hand they are sometimes surprisingly timid. The renowned 20th-century Swiss zoologist Charles Guggisberg recorded an incident in which a male lion, attracted by some antelope meat, entered a camp but accidentally pushed against a table on which had been placed an assortment of dishes and glassware. These rattled together noisily, whereupon the animal panicked and took off at high speed for a considerable distance. Indeed, when approaching lions on foot, often the major challenge is getting close enough for a good view and a photograph without them detecting you and disappearing into the bush.

My own first encounter with lions on foot was typical of this behaviour and represented a particularly inauspicious start to my time as a walking guide. We were in the Khwai River area of Botswana and had spotted a small group of lions resting comfortably under a tree. We drew lots to see which one of us trainee guides would be the chosen one to lead the approach and the long straw fell to me. I carefully planned and executed what I fondly imagined to be the perfect approach – only to find, when I emerged from cover ready to proclaim the ideal photo opportunity to admiring colleagues, that I couldn't identify the tree under which they had been lying. In any event when eventually I did, the beasts, tired of waiting, had pushed off in search of more interesting entertainment.

The now famous, sometimes infamous, phrase 'whatever you do don't run', quoted in Chapter 1, is used by many guides in their pre-trail briefing. This may have exceedingly important implications if the advice therein is ignored, as this tale by Bennet de Klerk relates. There are two stories by and about him in the book (one here, and the other in Chapter 4).

Life is not a matter of holding good cards, but of playing a poor hand well.

- Robert Louis Stevenson. Scottish novelist, poet and travel writer (1850–1894)

———————————————————

In Africa there is a type of silence that speaks louder than the loudest noise. But, being silence, it is heard only by those who have lived in the African Bush for long enough to understand its language. This type of silence, you will be told by hunter and soldier alike, is always a warning. And the price you pay for not heeding it, often, is death.

Such was the silence that, on that hot, dry November morning, caused me to halt my group of students. We were in a Tamboti forest in the wilderness area of the Pilanesberg. There were nine students, all training to become trail guides, the guides who can safely take tourists on guided walks in dangerous game areas, the 'dangerous game' being the elephant, lion, leopard, buffalo, both rhino species, hippopotamus and spotted hyena. They were about three quarters through their four-month course.

I motioned them to stay put in the relative safety of the Tamboti while I investigated the route ahead. Tamboti is a jealous sort of tree; grass and other plants do not grow easily in dense Tamboti stands. I left the forest and tried to plot a route, the silence by now deafening in my ears. To the north and east of the Tamboti there was thick grass and dense Black Thorn Acacia, to the southeast equally dense sickle bush. Black rhino country.

A Tamboti forest – a haunt of black rhino. *(Bennet de Klerk)*

Bennet's decision was to walk through the grassland. *(Bennet de Klerk)*

There are a few reasons why one should avoid walking unexpectedly into black rhino. Unlike white rhino, they are very inquisitive animals and like to investigate any sound, smell or movement. The problem is they are really GTi-turbo rhinos – very fast and agile. And there is a certain feeling of uneasiness when suddenly a 1,200-kilogram black rhino with two horns of nearly a metre apiece decides to investigate you, approaching at an alarmingly fast pace. This has led to them getting a somewhat unfair reputation of being aggressive. Another reason to be extra careful when dealing with them is that you do not ever want to have to shoot one on the trail. The black rhino is a critically endangered animal and most guides worth their salt would rather take a hit from one than shoot it. Probably.

For these reasons I chose to take the southerly route. The yellow thatch grass was really too tall, but it was open grassland. No chance of surprising a black rhino there. So with instructions to stay close to me and walk quietly,

I fetched the students and moved carefully into the open grassland. We progressed for about 70 metres when, suddenly, 20 metres ahead, a Harley Davidson started to 'rev' and a yellow bolt of lightning exploded from the grass straight towards us. The growl of an angry lioness is something that you cannot fully explain to someone who has not been exposed to it before. You feel it as much as you hear it. From seven metres – where she stopped to stand and swear at us – the earth around you, and your body, trembles with the sound as if you are standing in front of a speaker at a rock concert. You don't, however, feel like cheering much. There is a subtle, yet important, difference between a serious charge from an elephant, buffalo or rhino, and that of a lion. All of them could easily kill you; but it's what happens afterwards that makes the difference. Most people would like their relatives to have something to bury or cremate after your departure from this world. The other animals might kill you. The lion, having killed you, will then proceed to feast on you. This is not a comforting thought.

I engaged in some urgent conversation with the lioness, pointing out to her the obvious advantages of leaving quite soon rather than risk being shot. Scary as it was, I was pleased that the students had been offered a great learning opportunity. And then, somewhere to the left, another Harley started. A big one, this time. At times like this, you seem to observe the world in slow motion: his long, dark mane waving, his big, yellow eyes, filled with hatred, focused on my throat, the most magnificent male lion came charging through the long thatch grass. The earth vibrated with his growling. I spoke to him with far greater urgency than I had to his female companion and he stopped at 4 metres, continuing the conversation. It was not without some trepidation that I met, and maintained, his gaze. A 500-grain monolithic solid bullet was chambered in the CZ .458, and I took great pains explaining to him that we would both be far better off should he just call it a day and allow us to leave.

Somewhere in the course of my conversation with the big male, the lioness turned 90 degrees, faced east, and started roaring. She was calling in reinforcements … I had never seen this before. Meanwhile the male was standing his ground. One does experience a certain amount of inferiority whilst having a conversation of this nature despite the .458 rifle.

Suddenly, another Harley came rushing in, growling loudly as she did. Now I was facing two really grumpy lionesses at 7 metres, and a 230-kilogram male lion at less than 4 metres. What a learning opportunity for the students, I thought. You deal with a lion charge by facing them off, bullying back the bully. Safety lies in numbers. But something was wrong with this lion charge. Normally lions will charge, you face them and try talking some sense into them, then they back off, you back off, they charge again, you repeat the procedure and after a number of charges they decide it's OK and you leave, knees trembling. But not this time. Despite my best means of persuasion they would not back off. If anything they were inching ever closer.

What Bennet thought the lions saw. *(Bennet de Klerk)*

'Can't they count?' I found myself wondering. 'Ten of us, three of them …
never seen lions this brave before.' Then, suddenly, another Harley. She came
at great speed. A small tree close to me caused her to miss the reason for the
commotion and, as women do when all else fails, she sort of attacked the male,
gave him a smack. As he turned to scorn her, I saw the gap to start the retreat.
I turned my head to tell the students 'We can start …'

There was no-one there.

I felt, at that moment, exactly what Chief Seathl[3] had meant, two centuries
ago, by 'great loneliness of spirit'. You are very alone if four really angry lions,
metres away, are busy planning your demise – with not another human in
sight. I remember, vividly, thinking how these lions were probably saying to
themselves: 'Can't he count? Only himself, and four of us …'

There was no option. I had to start backing off. Slowly. Very slowly. The sights
of that .458 were straight between the eyes of the one with the black mane… but
there were four lions and only one rifle. My hat got hooked on a Black Thorn
Acacia, and I still fumbled to get it loose for a few moments before deciding to
leave it there – I paid seventy bucks for that hat, mind you! – and continued the
slow retreat. For about forty metres all four of them followed me step by step,
growling all the way. The two later arrivals then lay down but the male and the

---

3 Chief Seathl, a native American, was a Suquamish and Duwamish chief who pursued a path of
   accommodation to white settlers. The city of Seattle is named after him.

What the lions actually saw. *(Bennet de Klerk)*

first female followed me until I reached the Tamboti forest upon which they started pacing up and down, roaring and defecating until I was out of sight.

I did find the students again, much further back. As it turned out they had left – by no means slowly – even before the third lion arrived. Their main concern whilst waiting in the safety of the Tamboti was, apparently, who would retrieve the rifle from the feeding site and who would inform my wife of the manner of my demise. The latter, undoubtedly, would be the more dangerous encounter.

Even surprise, unplanned encounters such as this one generally end speedily and without significant incident, albeit often preceded by a warning growl or two which is most persuasive in generating an immediate though slow and careful withdrawal by the walking party. Lions are mostly interested in food, mating and avoiding their principal enemy, man. But when visitors are on foot, prides with cubs, lions on a kill (especially if they have just killed and are hungry) and, potentially, lions mating are generally scenarios to avoid wherever possible. It was a fair time after the event that Bennet discovered the reason for the lions' irascibility. On the other side of the area of long grass from which they'd emerged was a recent kill and some baby lions. The lodge guests at this wonderful sighting, having been sitting contentedly in their game drive

This lion pride of 13 includes cubs and a kill – a most dangerous
circumstance in which to disturb them.*(Maryann Williams)*

vehicle, probably are wondering to this day why the adult lions had pushed off away
from the kill into the grass and asking, 'What was all that growling about?'

Baby or very young lions can appear irresistibly cuddly, and walking alongside
them provides a very exciting experience for many visitors to Africa. Reading accounts
of these walks on social media only serves to reinforce the attraction and popularity.
But however careful the operators of these entertainments, there are risks involved, and
a number of instances have been documented of serious injury and at least one death
by mauling.

The following harrowing incident has a very different slant on the 'wild lion' bush
encounter, recounted to me with real understatement and honesty by a very young
guide, Liam Burrough, who showed extraordinary inventiveness and courage in what
became a desperate situation. Subsequently – and unsurprisingly to me and many
others – Liam went on to become not just an experienced but an extremely talented
professional who I have much enjoyed being guided by on a number of occasions.

May 2011, however, found Liam as a newly employed field guide with a week-old
basic guiding qualification and no experience to speak of. In keeping with the anxiety
that all newly qualified guides have about employment prospects he accepted the first
position he was offered, at a well-known game lodge renowned for taking on start-up
guides at reasonable salaries and offering guiding experience with the Big Five. He was
very excited: at last, his first taste of professional guiding!

In the lodge on the evening before his official start date Liam was told by the owner
that on the following morning he would be leading a walk with tourists into a Big Five

area accompanied by two lion cubs. Lion cubs? Furthermore he, who had never fired a rifle before, would be armed. This was a difficult moment for a 19-year-old who wanted both to express his concerns about this prospect and to remain in employment. So he most politely reminded the employer that he held neither a walking guide qualification nor an advanced rifle-handling certificate. The owner promptly dismissed his concerns and assured him that these were not necessary as the lodge was private property and that he as landowner could give all the relevant permissions.

Liam was handed a .416 rifle and five cartridges, and given a few basic instructions about loading. He told himself very firmly, more than once, that he wouldn't have to use

Liam Burrough with his not-so-baby lion. (*Liam Burrough*)

it but that the guests would be much reassured by its existence. The action plan for the day was simple. Wake up the guests, switch on the coffee machine, walk down to the enclosure where the lion cubs were kept, release them and bring them up to the lodge. There, outside the entrance, he would then brief the guests on the bush walk.

Morning broke bright and sunny – far sunnier than he felt – but after the essential preliminaries in the lodge he strolled down along a diamond-mesh fence towards the cubs' home, trying to appear nonchalant about the whole business. Dominate the cubs, show them he meant business: that should do the trick. However, when he arrived at the creaking, rusty gate of an enclosure he was greeted with something that stopped him in his tracks. Before him stood a sub-adult lion and lioness looking very interested at the possibility of an outing. Had he made a wrong turn? There must be another enclosure. These weren't cubs – they were a good 16 months old. He checked with a passing and distinctly uninterested gardener, who assured him that this was indeed the right place and they were certainly the lions that went for a walk with guests. His parting words 'they are no longer cubs', did absolutely nothing to enhance Liam's confidence.

By this time the lions had become rather boisterous, clearly ready for the off, and after Liam nervously opened the gate he had to use a decent bit of strength and balance to keep them from knocking him to the ground with that characteristic greeting ceremony of pushing and leaning that lions are known for. Of course, they knew the routine by heart after months of almost daily walks, and made a bee-line for the lodge where guests were already waiting.

The back-up guide for the walk, also unqualified, gave some prompts with regard to the rules of the game for the guests, which included no running, no shouting, no separating from the group and absolutely no crouching down, all of which might attract unwanted responses from the adolescent cats, such as playfully jumping up or even gentle biting. Feeling very nervous but somewhat reassured by the eagerness of the guests, the back-up and the lions, Liam delivered the briefing in the most confident style he could manage and loaded a few rounds into the magazine of the weapon, and the gallant band proceeded to leave the lodge grounds and enter the surrounding wilderness.

For the first 45 minutes or so all seemed to go really well. The cubs were full of energy and raced amongst the grewia bushes, seemingly oblivious to the camera-swinging onlookers as the party made its way down well-trodden paths. By now Liam's confidence was rising and he recalled some interesting things to tell the group about knobthorn trees. A fleeting glimpse of an impala offered another opportunity to entertain the guests, and the discussion that he triggered by identifying a leopard track (albeit rather old) all added to his feeling of well-being.

Suddenly the morning peace was disturbed by a commotion behind and to his right. Liam spun around and was faced with a terrifying sight. A young woman had broken off from the group to take a photograph, had been hooked by a buffalo thorn bush and had dropped her expensive Nikon. She squealed with dismay and bent over to pick up the camera. This triggered an instantaneous response from the lioness, who raced over towards her and leapt onto her back.

In a split second the woman was flat on her face under the cat, who seemed at that stage only intent on pinning her to the ground. Liam raced towards the scene and mid-stride yelled, 'Lie still, we'll get her off!' – but already it was too late: understandably the guest had panicked and was screaming and struggling. Presumably this served to further encourage the predatory response because the cat latched firmly onto the woman's neck and face with her formidable claws and bit into the back of her skull.

Blood ran down the animal's forelegs, saturating the lady's clothing as well as the underlying grass, and she let out a terrified scream that reinforced the seriousness of her situation. At this point the male lion raced forward to join the party, but a swift kick in his direction sent him round in a circle with the cowed expression of a scolded dog. He lunged forward with a paw, snagged the camera, which was a short distance from the woman, and bolted to the cover of a raisin bush with his prize.

Liam's first attempt at rescue was to try and kick the lioness off the guest. He admitted to me later that he was not a very athletic chap, but his first mighty swing landed fair and square on the side of the lioness's head. No reaction whatsoever. Nothing. After all, lions are tough creatures and frequently sustain blunt trauma from prey such as buffalo and giraffe that are far more powerful than a skinny Zimbabwean guide. So he kicked her again, hard, as hard as he could, though this further even more vigorous effort was less accurate, the boot finding only the side of the guest's head. Tourists are not as tough as lions and this instantly rendered the woman unconscious. This might have been more a blessing than a disaster as she ceased struggling and fell silent.

Evidently, a change of tactics was required. So the next step involved using the butt of the rifle in similar fashion, but this produced possessive growling from the lioness who was now content with the near-complete success of her kill. So Liam made the regrettable, but by then inevitable, decision to permanently terminate the animal's contract of employment.

He chambered around and shouted to the guests to get behind him as he was going to shoot. Standard practice. One round up and forward into the chamber. He aimed generally at the lioness's skull, took a deep breath and slid his finger into the trigger guard. But, staring through the open sights of the .416 he suddenly realised that things had become more complicated and much more serious. The lioness had taken the by now very limp guest's head into her mouth, and a point-blank shot would undoubtedly travel through the head of both cat and victim. So he swung the weapon down and aimed for a chest shot, but the lioness lifted the front half of the woman's body with her strong forequarters and began to drag her off into the bushes. After all, that's what lions do.

Liam was out of ideas. But then, through this by now well-established panic, something came to him: a seed of memory rapidly germinating. Just a week before he'd watched a nature programme in which a surfer had survived a shark attack by pushing his thumbs into the predator's eyes. Hell, at this point what other options were there? He threw the weapon onto the ground, jumped astride the lioness like mounting a miniature horse, gripped her shoulders with his thighs, latched onto her lower jaw with both hands and pressed into the rear of her eye sockets with his thumbs.

That did the trick. She struggled for a moment beneath him but then released the woman, leapt from his grip and ran to the clump of bush where her brother had hidden with the now completely disassembled Nikon. Liam was not just unhorsed but thrown backwards to the ground. He scrambled forward to try and help the now very bloodied guest, who was still lying face down in the grass. She was unconscious and blood was pouring from a substantial wound on the back of her scalp as well as countless puncture wounds on the chin, jawline and neck. At this point the back-up guide joined in, and together they put pressure on the largest wounds with their hands as they tried pull the still limp victim to her feet before the lioness regained sufficient courage to try and reclaim her prize. She skulked around in the grass a bit and then suddenly rushed back towards them. Liam yelled and kicked to keep her at bay but, just at the moment he thought they were going to lose the battle, a game drive vehicle, alerted by all the commotion, arrived on the scene, and that made all the difference. Numbers count with lions. The guests, including the unfortunate victim, were loaded into the vehicle and driven speedily to the lodge. From there the lady was evacuated to the nearest large private hospital, two hours' drive away. Amazingly, she suffered no dangerous or permanent physical damage from what must have been a terrifying experience.

They don't walk lions at that lodge any more!

Try putting the phrase 'Walking with lions, South Africa' in your search engine and a large number of tourist opportunities will flash up on the screen. A quick scan of the contents will reveal that, in the main, those who took up the chance to participate in such an activity found it highly enjoyable and informative, and sometimes the highlight of their African holiday. But from a conservation point of view it's much, much more complex. Firstly the experience may suggest to tourists that lions can be habituated to humans and then are not dangerous. But their instincts, whilst usually dormant, can be reawakened in a flash and lead to an incident such as that described above.

Much less obvious, and given much less publicity, is the question that should be asked of those businesses that invite volunteers to work and visitors to pay in lion-walking enterprises that are far bigger than the lodge Liam described. The cubs may have been removed from their mothers, who are rarely wild lions themselves, at a very young age, two to three weeks. This is contrary to nature and one has to ask whether this simply is a device to bring the mothers back into oestrus, the breeding state (which it does). A more difficult question is what happens to the cubs when they are much older. After habituation to humans for over a year the possibility of reintroduction to the wild – always assuming someone will take them – is remote and very rarely documented. The famous Elsa written about by Joy Adamson is an unusual circumstance. So what happens to the cubs? There are limited options. Euthanasia? Sold off to hunting concessions of one kind or another? Think about it.

* * *

Polite Zwelile is a Zulu tracker who had the most extraordinary and, after the dust had literally settled, fascinating close encounter with a lioness. It's quite easy from the comfort of an armchair to say that it shouldn't really have happened, but that isn't the way it is in the bush.

Sitting on the tracker's seat at the front end of the game drive vehicle, he and his guide, who was driving, had espied a pair of lions mating in some thick bushes about 100 metres away. The fact that the guests aboard had never seen lions before may have acted as a spur to a closer approach, but the majority of guides would have done so anyway. The act is rather infrequently observed, and most people are keen to see exactly what happens. There is no guarantee of privacy for mating animals in the bush.

As they got closer, about 30 metres from the lions, it became clear that there was a significant obstacle to manoeuvring the vehicle to the optimal position for a good view and some photographs. This obstacle took the form of a pile of logs lying transversely across their approach path. It would be useful, suggested the guide, if Polite could lean over and try to move the logs. So he did. Unfortunately this didn't work out quite as planned. As he tried to wrench one of the logs out of the way he overbalanced and fell off the tracker's seat onto the ground. When he rose to a crouching position, he was

How Polite Zwelile remembers his lioness. (*Patricia Goodwin*)

more than a little startled to see the lioness of the couple standing in front of him, just a metre away. The only thing separating them was a couple of the dead branches on the ground. She looked directly at him and growled angrily and noisily. This was, he thought, the end.

Automatically, without any sort of conscious thought process, he spoke gently to her. 'We're only here to take photographs. We didn't want to disturb you.' Polite by name and polite by nature. Later he reflected that in effect he was pleading for his life. She seemed unimpressed and growled loudly again. But then there was a very soft growl from the male lion who hadn't moved except to sit upright and watch the proceedings at the vehicle. Immediately the female retreated about 5 metres though still watching Polite. Taking advantage of the increasing gap between them he hauled himself up, almost jumping backwards, onto his tracker's seat. This provoked another rush from the lioness, back to where she had been – close, much too close, to him. But once again the male lion growled, still gently. And once again the lioness retreated, but this time all the way. The incident was closed.

This very brief but dramatic incident poses an interesting question. Did the male lion's soft growl in any way influence the female's retreat from her confrontation with Polite? Or was it just coincidence? We know that many animals communicate verbally with others of the same species, sometimes extensively, though frequently we have only minimal comprehension. Whilst there is always a temptation to be anthropomorphic and ascribe the meaning of a specific call to a human-type response, it is equally inappropriate to write events such as this off as coincidence. So when we mull over Polite's adventure the truth is that we don't know why it turned out that way.

3 DAGHA BOYS

Upon arrival at camp, clients spend the first three days of their trip learning the basic elements of buffalo hunting: running, climbing, rapid reloading and praying, with the major emphasis on invocation of the Deity.

- Peter Hathaway Capstick, American hunter and author (1940–1996)

Big, aggressive and potentially bad-tempered – a dagha boy. *(Sharon Haussmann)*

There comes a time in the life of a male buffalo when he becomes old, thick-bossed[4] and almost hairless. Buffalo bulls have a reputation for being irritable and aggressive. Indeed, it is said that an old buffalo is the only animal that looks at you as if you owe him money. These old guys, if encountered alone or in very small groups when on foot in the bush, prompt serious concern amongst guides. They are known colloquially as 'dagha boys'. 'Dagha' is a word derived from the Zulu and Xhosa languages for building mortar made largely from mud and sometimes cow-dung, so it relates to the fact that these old and increasingly hairless animals often coat themselves with mud by wallowing, as protection from sun damage, overheating and possibly parasites. They have constructed a deserved reputation as formidable and dangerous opponents.

James Stevenson-Hamilton, the first warden of the Kruger National Park, considered them to be the

> most dangerous of creatures to take liberties with. They are far tougher than lions, and far more solidly determined to get even with an enemy. In fact a wounded buffalo will hunt his tormentor much as a terrier does a rat.

He was not alone in these views. The famous hunter Frederick Selous had much the same view. He said:

> I know of several instances where buffaloes have charged suddenly and apparently in unprovoked ferocity upon people who never even saw them until they were dashed, in many cases mortally wounded, to the ground: but I believe that, in any rate the majority of cases … these buffaloes would be found to have been previously wounded by some other hunter.

The sum of all this suggests: 'Old male buffalo, bad. Old wounded male buffalo, very, very bad.'

Chris Green, an experienced walking guide, wrote down most of this story on a Sunday evening just two weeks after the buffalo hit him. He told me that at the time it was really an odd feeling to be alive and walking when he knew that many people damaged by a charging buffalo do not survive and those that do mostly have horrific injuries. He'd got away comparatively lightly, with two fractured ribs, some other rib and chest problems and a compression injury to a thoracic vertebra. Even when we spoke, many years later, his spine was still very tender and clicked whenever he turned onto his side. He was still unable to lie on his belly, and had a few residual scars on his head and torso too. The story went like this.

It was a nice September day in the Lowveld with fluffy white clouds scattered through a wash of pale blue. There were three on the walk, a route that Chris had done many times before: with him were Donald, an experienced guide, and Mike, a guest. The terrain over which they were walking was very varied, with cliffs standing grandly above a sandy riverbed and deep riverine thickets that were best avoided – unpleasant things might

---

4 The bases of the curving horns of the male African buffalo come very close together and often fuse to form a shield-like protuberance known as a 'boss'.

lurk there! A critical moment was to leave the riverbed and cross a small spur through thorn bushes that opened out into a sparsely tree-covered slope with decent visibility of 50 metres or so. Walking up across a spur is always awkward in the bush, as you have no visibility of what may lie over the top on the level ground that lies beyond. In this instance it was fine, but the devil is always in the detail – the detail in this case being that there were in this area of decent visibility, as there usually are, and some bushes and thickets which were denser than others. The chance of something big and dangerous being concealed within these is small but can happen. And this time it did.

The old male buffalo burst out from behind a small shrub and was at full speed by the time Chris got a clear view of him. His first impression was that the animal didn't appear to know where his potential victims were, so he might be able to take cover behind some thin shrubs. As he did so he chambered a round into the breech of his rifle. But he could hear the buffalo coming on very fast so he turned to shoot, only to find the animal just one pace away. So with the rifle at hip height he tried, but failed, to get the shot off and was instantly cartwheeled back and to the side, the buffalo catching his head on the way down.

There followed an incredibly rapid and weirdly painless buffeting and bashing and tumbling until he found himself lying on his right side with the apparently enraged buffalo hitting his lower legs and knees from behind and screwing his boss into them. Then the animal turned and came around to the other side to continue. In the beginning Chris had recalled that this was a buffalo and that most people get killed when it pushes through with the charge. But now he had a surreal and detached thought that everything was fine and the buffalo was welcome to bash away at his feet. In reality, by this time he was in a bad way. He was finding it difficult to breathe and he was bleeding profusely from somewhere on his head, so much so that his eyes seemed to be filled with a red paste of some kind. Then the buffalo stopped the attack abruptly. Who knows why? Chris was choking whilst trying to vomit and breathe at the same time. Was this it? Trying to lift his head and support it with his forearm was impossible – his neck had already started to stiffen, his body felt numb and his head felt heavy. Was this really the end?

It took a massive effort to look to the side and backwards, and even then he couldn't see very far. But he was acutely aware of a huge shape standing, head lowered, not 2 metres away. Its breathing was short and sharp in puffs. Until then Chris hadn't really heard the animal at all and could only surmise that his own laboured breathing and the stress of the whole episode had masked any extraneous sounds until the moment when the attack stopped. The realisation that the bull was still there and waiting for any movement on Chris's part was a terrifying moment. Any respite was probably going to be short-lived, as the buffalo probably hadn't finished yet. Almost at the same time the animal gave a snort and delivered a huge blow to Chris's lower back. He felt himself being lifted and moved forward in the air, and as soon as he hit the ground the buffalo hit him in the back yet again with terrible force, screwing his boss into the centre of Chris's spine, then shifting to the space between the shoulder blades and really pushing hard. Chris said to himself – possibly even shouted – 'Oh no!' and arched his back, letting out what air had been in his lungs. This, he now decided, was probably close to the end of his life and if the buffalo started to stamp on him and kick him any more there would no avoiding it. At this point Chris decided that playing dead was the only option left open to him. Maybe the noisy expulsion of breath, the unnatural posture and immobility together would convince the buffalo that he was dead.

It shouldn't be all that difficult, he thought. In truth he couldn't move much and he was in great pain. Possibly he was near to death anyway. But after this rush of awful thoughts, the buffalo broke off the assault and retreated in stages, pausing at about 5-metre intervals until he was 50–60 metres away. At this point he destroyed a couple of small bushes with his horns, urinated, defaecated and moved on.

Then things happened very quickly. Immediately after the buffalo had decided that enough was enough, Donald, who'd managed to smuggle the guest with him and out of sight behind a tree, called softly suggesting that Chris should stay put, as he was unsure of the precise location of the buffalo. This seemed an extremely good idea, given that Chris wasn't sure if he could get up or indeed move much at all. Donald dispatched Mike up a tree both for safety and to act as a spotter, and came over to where Chris was lying.

'Ah, Jesus Chris, are you all right? I'll get you out of here.' He carefully checked the fallen rifle, and at that point Chris unaccountably felt that he was probably just winded. Indeed, all he needed was some water to rinse out his eyes. But that idea was quickly dispelled. As soon as he tried to get up he developed dramatic respiratory distress. They had a mobile phone – and, miraculously, a signal – so Donald was able to call for help and at some point in the ensuing discussion it was agreed that a helicopter was unnecessary. In hindsight this was a poor call and it would have been infinitely more comfortable and probably medically safer than the subsequent vehicle extraction.

The evacuation was tough. They managed to get Chris to his feet and, supporting him all the time, the little group made literally agonisingly slow progress on foot until, blessedly, a camp vehicle hove into sight. Chris looked a real mess. Blood dripped freely from somewhere on his head, mud and dust covered most of his body, and his shirt was in tatters. From camp, the first part of the journey, in the front of a double-cab to hospital in Hoedspruit, the nearest town with a medical facility, was long and extremely painful. Chris describes the subsequent ambulance ride as almost as bad. But eventually he arrived and was admitted. After the usual assessment and arrangements for monitoring, an unexpected but welcome treat appeared; a cup of tea. Presumably the staff had already decided that surgery was unnecessary. Apart from an occasional flurry of interest in his blood pressure, which was quite unstable for a while, and a journey to another hospital for more sophisticated x-rays, the rest of his hospital stay was uneventful. But recovery took a long time and was accompanied by significant pain for quite a while. It took over a month for him to get back to work.

Postscript:

Soon after the incident the local game warden with his trackers went back to the scene and located the animal about a kilometre from the scene of the incident. He was recognised as the same buffalo that had nearly killed a game scout in a similar attack a month or so earlier, identified by the broken tips of his horns and worn patches on his hide, which gave him a generally dishevelled appearance. Both of the victims had seen these details whilst lying on the ground. The old buff was truly in a bad way. He had an abscess on his neck and was blind in one eye. In addition he had no front teeth so feeding must have become a real problem. No wonder he was short-tempered. He'd chosen a good hide-out with water only 500 metres away, some good sweetveld grazing and raised ground – a spot with good observation and easy to defend. The decision to kill an animal is never taken lightly but in this circumstance it was a humane act.

Chris talks very honestly of going through a type of post-traumatic stress phase which, apart from a depressive component, included a perpetual and frequently verbalised disbelief that he had actually survived with comparatively minor injuries. This was associated with the idea that he didn't deserve to survive, together with a concomitant self-critical feeling that he should have seen the buffalo sooner. Maybe fitness and good general health were important factors in his fairly speedy recovery, but Chris believes that the care given by his wife Penny was what turned the tide. She had a great deal to put up with during the difficult recovery period, sometimes lying awake wondering if he was going to breathe his last. He still believes he was very, very lucky.

Some guide mentors remind their trainees that there are three top tips for walking in the bush. The first is to stay focused at all times; the second is to stay focused at all times and I won't bore you with the third. This always reminds me of a great story related to me a few years ago whilst I was in the Maasai Mara by the main participant. If this was a Sherlock Holmes story it would be entitled 'The Adventure of the Plastic Bottle'.

It was a sunny, warm and clear-skied August morning when Douglas Nagi, a senior and highly experienced guide in Kenya, set off from the lodge where he worked in the south-east corner of the Maasai Mara, to take two American guests to the airstrip to begin their return trip to the States.

As is the convention, unless timings are tight it is as much game drive as passenger transport. The first part of the journey was across the rolling, bush-studded hills typical of the concession and that area of the Mara National Reserve. It was migration time and hordes of wildebeest, zebra, Thomson's gazelle and a surprisingly significant number of eland were milling around or forming those classic long, winding columns as they readied themselves for the big moment of the Mara crossing. There were frequent stops for yet more photographs, and they spent some time with two big male lions and six females from a large group of lions called the Henry Pride. There was nothing particularly dramatic, but it demanded the usual concentration on everything from the sometimes difficult road, to looking out for other animals and assessing the best angle for camera shots. Douglas had done the trip hundreds of times before, so it was easy to arrive at the airstrip a few minutes before the scheduled departure time without too much stress. No punctures either, thank goodness.

Douglas Nagi telling his story. *(Maryann Williams)*

The Kenya Airways Twin Otter took off easily, showing off its short strip capabilities so essential in this part of the world, and Douglas set off back to camp. It was an easy, non-taxing, familiar journey of well under two hours without stops. Probably, it was a combination of this familiarity and the more relaxed situation of a client-free drive that brought about near-disaster.

About 30 minutes from home he received a call on his mobile phone from a great friend in Nairobi. The friend had been to a most splendid and eventful party the night before and was anxious to share, in some detail, the amazing fun that everyone had experienced. Except for Douglas of course, who had been on duty and unable to attend. It was during this conversation that he noticed a discarded plastic drinks bottle some 25–30 metres away from the vehicle on the right-hand side. In common with many others, the lodge policy was very specific about plastic waste, so he stopped the vehicle and got out. Here was grassland dotted quite profusely with magic guarri bushes:[5] evergreen, dense and tall enough to hide animals – large animals, sort of buffalo-sized

<hr />

5 Magic Guarri (*Euclea divinorum*) is a bush of the *Ebenaceae* (Ebony) family made famous by its reputation as the source of branches for divining water. It can grow to a height of 8 metres.

animals. But, with the mobile phone still held firmly to his ear, his mind was more focused on social chat and garbage retrieval than on potential dangers in the bush. So it wasn't until he bent to retrieve the bottle and then looked up that he saw fate in the shape of a very large dagha boy bearing down on him at high speed.

When the old chap emerged from behind the bush he didn't hesitate for an instant but came racing towards the human intruder in his space. Douglas didn't hesitate either but turned on his heel and dashed for the vehicle at what he later believed to be Olympian speed, dropping the bottle and his mobile in the process. It wasn't fast enough. Hoofbeats pounded up behind, closing rapidly. He wasn't going to reach the vehicle, let alone get in and shut the still-open door. So, at the last moment he swerved dramatically to the right and dashed around the front of the vehicle and down the passenger side whilst the buffalo, surprised by the manoeuvre, skidded almost to a halt, much as they do in animal cartoons, before continuing the pursuit. But the sudden change of direction slowed him up enough for Douglas to vault the passenger-side door, climb into the driver's seat and close that door. This was a feat of physical agility that he would never be able to repeat in normal circumstances. Realising that he'd lost the race, the buffalo became enraged and charged the vehicle from the front. Douglas started the engine and it immediately stalled, which usually happens only in bad movies. The animal charged again, this time bending the bull-bar to an extraordinary degree. But the engine re-start alarmed him and he ran off, leaving Douglas to accelerate rapidly away and avoid further damage.

By the time he reached the lodge, fear – and its regular partner, the adrenaline rush – had been replaced by anger and hurt professional pride. Revenge of an extremely violent nature was clearly the answer. So, equipped with a .458 and accompanied by a couple of Maasai colleagues with a spear and a bow and arrows, he set off on a quest for his mobile phone and retribution, not necessarily in that order. Of course, they never found the buffalo, and in any case tempers had cooled and so by that time he'd earned a reprieve. But Douglas did get back his phone, lying on the ground where he'd dropped it and entirely undamaged. Mysteriously, the plastic bottle could not be located. Perhaps the buffalo took it.

It's worth reminding ourselves that not all sick or wounded fully grown male buffaloes are hostile to walking groups. This takes me back a few years when, on the first day of my two-day assessment to be a walking guide, I was leading a group of trainee guides along a track which at that point had moderately thick woodland on both sides, encouragingly fully equipped with climbable trees. Rounding a bend we encountered a very large male buffalo some 50 metres ahead, grazing on the roadside grass. Although he had an impressive boss, his residual hair was not quite sufficient for him qualify as a dagha boy, but in any event he had to be considered a potential threat to anyone on foot. We stopped. He stared. Stared very intently indeed, but made no move towards us. So no fright and no flight by either party.

For our part we squatted down at the side of the track and talked a bit about the buffalo and the issues of 'what to do if …' He offered us an occasional glare but otherwise seemed pretty relaxed. I pointed out that this isn't what you always expect from a mature bull on his own, who would usually trot towards you with varying degrees of menace or, more likely, run away into cover. This behaviour suggested something else was afoot. Could he be ill or injured? There was only one way to find out, so I left the trainees with the back-up guide and walked slowly towards the buffalo. This walk re-defined the word 'slowly': indeed, observers might have been forgiven for thinking that I was not moving at all. At 25 metres from him it became clear that he was a sick guy; any movement seemed hesitant and awkward. When he half-turned away, my binoculars showed was evidence of old dark blood on his upper left hind leg and a suggestion of a significant wound above it. Most likely this was a war wound following a confrontation with another bull or possibly a result of an attack by a predator. In any event he ignored me and I retreated, still respectfully slowly, to the group, and we continued our walk, though giving him a wide berth. Later we radioed the reserve management in case veterinary assistance was required, but I never learned the outcome.

Aside from cantankerous old boys, buffaloes are generally shy and retiring animals, but in a herd they can still, albeit unwittingly, bring about dangerous situations. If something surprises them they may stampede en masse and more or less blindly. If you are in the way this presents a serious risk, particularly as they may suddenly turn about-face and charge back the way they came. Good acceleration, strong legs and handy trees may be important for those on foot who are unexpectedly exposed to that kind of crisis. Even in a vehicle there is a need for thoughtfulness when around these guys, and the following non-walking tale, of an event which happened to a guide acquaintance of mine, Jacques Briam, is included just in case vehicle-borne ventures seem deceptively straightforward.

That evening just after dark, the game drive had suddenly become much more interesting. There was the usual chatter on the radio net, everyone telling everyone else where they were and what they'd seen. One of the other vehicles, which had just started its nocturnal exploration of the bush after the traditional stop for sundowners, had come across two lionesses walking with apparent intent and was following them. If the animals maintained the same direction they would march slap bang into a herd of buffalo that they'd found that afternoon. Indeed, it soon became clear that their plan was to do just that. They were walking with great deliberation in an almost straight line so, on hearing this encouraging news, Jacques and his guide colleague moved their vehicle into a decent position to see any action that might ensue.

Events moved quickly. The lions closed up on the buffalo herd and the herd scattered. Immediately, the guides heard the wailing noise commonly heard when an animal is in distress, so drove along a track and then off-road to see what we presumed was a kill. They got close enough to see that the lionesses had pulled down a sub-adult buffalo and had gathered around to commence their nutritional reward. One of the advantages of being vehicle-borne is that you can get quite close to this sort of event, particularly in the dark when being on foot is out of the question. Even in daylight this wouldn't be a place to walk.

As there was no tracker on board, Jacques had elected to perch on the little seat that trackers use that is fixed on the front left-hand side of the bonnet. It's a good place for swinging the lamp on night drives. It's also a place where, at times, one can feel rather exposed, especially if very large animals like elephants approach closely. So there they were, spotlight illuminating the scene for the guests, and everyone both fascinated and excited.

Now when the lions attacked the buffalo herd had panicked and split into two groups, dispersing left and right, but they actually hadn't gone very far. So what happened next was almost predictable and entirely spectacular. The buffalos counter-

Memo to self – when very close to dangerous animals don't ride on the tracker seat. *(Jeff Williams)*

attacked. They came charging in, all noise and dust, and in the process rather than deliberately, charged the vehicle as well as the lions. Unfortunately, one of the first things that they damaged was Jacques' leg. A large buffalo horn scored a direct hit on one of his legs, which had been dangling down in front of him. Fortunately it was more of a glancing blow than a direct hit, otherwise, instead of just being cut and badly bruised, the whole lower part of his leg would have been a write-off.

The vehicle backed off quickly. The guests had their photographs, one of them had managed to get ultra-dramatic video footage, and the guides had had plenty enough excitement for the night. The lions did the sensible thing and made a sharp exit, though they may well have returned later to dispute the rights to the remaining food with the almost inevitable bunch of marauding spotted hyaenas.

4 A PLACE CALLED LEEUWFONTEIN

I have spent a lot of time walking in Pilanesberg National Park. There are, as in most parks, clearly specified and delineated areas where guided walking is allowed, so you get to know them pretty well. One such area is 'Scary Leeuwfontein', so-named for being well known to all the guides in the park for having a history of incidents. Probably this is because the bush is very thick, and an extremely popular haunt of black rhinos and sometimes buffaloes. Mind you, as there's a great chance of seeing lots of interesting stuff in the area it's a very attractive and popular place to go – and the more you go somewhere the more you get incidents there.

The Euphorbia tree (*Euphorbia ingens*): toxic to humans but prized by black rhinos. (*Patricia Goodwin*)

On one occasion we were completing a three-hour walk at Leeuwfontein looking for anything that turned up, though particularly encounters with dangerous animals. Although one should never give up on the bush, we had just begun to believe that this was not our day when, out of the blue – 'contact!' Some 50 metres ahead stood a black rhino bull, out in the open, feeding on a fallen candelabra tree (*Euphorbia ingens*). The wind was unfavourable, so he caught our scent immediately and ran off at 90 degrees left to our line of march and into cover. It had been a good sighting, albeit briefer than we might have wished. But in any event the Euphorbia made a great discussion topic and we lingered awhile, dwelling largely on things botanical. The milky latex (or sap) of *Euphorbia ingens* is potentially very poisonous to humans especially, producing severe skin irritation and even blindness. Most herbivores also avoid the tree. Not so, however, the black rhino or baboon or vervet monkey. They like it, and derive water from it in times of drought.

Ten minutes passed and then we were ready to continue the walk. The back-up guide was moving back to the group having been ably fulfilling his rôle by acting as lookout whilst we talked. As he did so his 360-degree visual sweep passed across the path we had taken to reach where we now stood. There, standing astride our path and staring at us, stood our very own black rhino bull. He was just beginning to walk slowly towards us when we adjusted our formation, armed lead guide to the fore and the rest behind. Not a problem at this stage, no round chambered, just a watching brief. The rhino, recognising that the game was up, ambled gently off into cover.

He did not behave aggressively. He had circled and emerged behind us. Was this accidental or deliberate? He saw us, we moved, he left. Some would say that he pushed off because he recognised force majeure, but we believed he was curious. Not idle curiosity but a simple tactic to check where we were, what we were doing and where we were going. A necessary intelligence gathering operation as part of his defensive strategy. One must never take a black rhino (or any other animal) for granted, and never underestimate their potential for causing significant injury. But please, let's not invariably apply to them the label of the ogre of the thick bush, as sometimes they are portrayed.

It would be absolutely incorrect to think that every walk in this area would bring unparalleled adventure and seriously scary moments. But its topography and its famous thickets attract animals, so there's a good chance of encountering something. The next two stories also took place in this same area. The first is by Bennet de Klerk, who we have already met. As before, I have retained his telling of the tale in the first person:

July, 1999. I have three guests on trail; my back-up, Doug, was quite experienced. The venue, Leeuwfontein. An area where you really need to stay focused: Dense, much frequented by black rhino and on a major elephant and lion route. As Uncle Scar told young Simba about the elephant graveyard: 'Only the bravest lions go there.'

We have a great walk with lovely birds, interesting tracks and signs, nice zebra, a few white rhino grazing peacefully. But the walk, as my walks tend to,

One of the many thickets at Leeuwfontein. *(Jeff Williams)*

lingers and time passes. 'We do', the husband tells me suddenly, 'have a flight to catch'.

Oops. It's at least a 40-minute walk back to the vehicle. Too long.

Unless …

There is that thicket. We can save a good 20 minutes by taking a short cut through the thicket. Not advisable of course but hey, I was younger then and less risk averse. The thicket it would be!

The guests are briefed again – stay close, walk quietly in single file, react immediately to commands if anything happens.

Less than 100m into the thicket one of the trails guide's scariest sounds erupts, about 30m ahead of me on the path. Not dissimilar to a horse sneezing; a short airy snort. A snort that shoots right through your liver in situations like this: the alarm snort of a black rhino. Almost at the same moment I see the bull raising itself from its shady resting place under a mountain karee where he'd been snoozing. I heard Doug moving the guests out. Fast, efficient, no running, into cover. As lead guide I need to stand my ground, be the barrier between animal and guest. Having a good back-up in a situation like this takes off a lot of the pressure. I know the guests are safe.

In seconds the bull halves the distance to me, stops, sniffs the air. He doesn't know where or what I am; the wind isn't in his favour. But he is going to find out.

Today, two decades of experience later, I might have handled the situation differently. I have learned that black rhino, contrary to their reputation, are not really aggressive. They are, however, very curious. Very curious indeed and one can be forgiven for feeling quite vulnerable when, at Usain Bolt speed, a 1-ton beast with two formidable weapons on its nose comes to investigate what's up. More often than not, immediately identifying yourself and talking calmly satisfies the curiosity.

But, back in 1999, I thought it best to hide. So there I was, cuddled up to a raisin bush, frozen to the spot with the rhino making short, five paces long, investigative rushes. So every rush brought him five paces closer. Across my legs lay my rifle; useless metal and wood given that my own little rule was never, ever, chamber a round in a 'rhino situation'. I had absolutely no idea what to do next. No plan. I knew that just three investigations further he would be right on top of me. And twelve kilometres away back at the lodge, tucked up in his cradle, lay three months old Casper, my son. I saw his little face and knew that he would grow up without having ever known his father. I really didn't have any idea how to handle the situation that had evolved over less than thirty seconds.

Another rush forward. Ten paces away. Then another – now it was five. Clearly, the next rush would be my crush. I could see clearly the bristles on his lip, the hollows of the follicles, his nostrils trembling. Those few seconds seemed like many minutes, hopeless ones. Far to the east a Natal Francolin called forlornly. Often dubbed the 'heart attack bird' by trails guides, these birds (now called Natal Spurfowl) have a habit of sitting tight until you are about to step on them before almost literally exploding from cover, at the same time making a massive noise. Almost enough to justify their nickname. The Bush, seconds before I should have been mauled, had told me what to do.

I exploded from my cover, shouting loudly, rushing right through the raisin bush haven. As I glanced over my shoulder I could only see the curled tail of the bull as he, too, rushed off – in the opposite direction. My knees were shaking profusely for at least forty minutes afterwards and the guests missed their flight. But I listened to the Bush. And lived.

Simply being in the wrong place at the wrong time happens to people all the time. A nurse colleague of mine was killed outright when a goods vehicle, coming in the opposite direction, flicked up a cats-eye from the centre of the road that smashed through the windscreen of the car she was driving. Even more dramatically personal for me, in another life a long time ago and far away, was the incident in which a sniper killed a young soldier who was standing right next to me during a particularly unpleasant riot. He, poor chap, could certainly claim the same thing. These 'wrong time, wrong place' events happen in the bush too, frequently associated with 'incidents'. Eugene Le Roux's story is a good example of a typical scenario in which from beginning to end the guide's decisions and conduct were exemplary and there was nothing more that could have done that would have affected the outcome. Both as tourist and guide in training I have walked with many highly experienced, highly competent guides. Eugene is one of a handful that I would, literally, follow anywhere.

It was a typical Highveld morning, pretty cool, when Eugene left the lodge just before sunrise, but with a promise of hotter things to come by late morning. Both he and his colleague Shaun were both fully fledged lead trails guides, but Eugene was the designated lead for the day and so it was his job to tell the North-West Parks Board administration which area they'd be going to and that the party consisted of two guides and five guests. They had selected an area of the park called Leeuwfontein for their walk, and this had two particular attractions: firstly they wouldn't have to waste time driving too far from the lodge and, more importantly, there was a really good chance of seeing some action in terms of sightings of some of the major animals in the park. In the event it turned out to be more action-rich than any of them had bargained for.

After parking the vehicle, loading the rifles and disembarking the guests the guides did the safety briefing. It's a routine part of every bush walk, and vitally important. In Leeuwfontein they normally start by avoiding the thickets, which can contain all manner of excitement far too early into the walk, and skirt them to the south before moving up onto a small area of raised ground called Euphorbia Hill. This was the route they took on the day. In truth the name of the hill is a misnomer. More a spur, it has never been a hill, and the euphorbias that once adorned it are long gone. But to call it

Euphorbia Hill, the site of Eugene LeRoux's elephant encounter.
The tree where we always sit is in the red circle. (*Jeff Williams*)

An elephant breeding herd. Mothers with their offspring are
unpredictable and potentially extremely dangerous. *(Patricia Goodwin)*

Spur innominata or some other name would be churlish and an insult to history. So
Euphorbia Hill it remains, and it is a most pleasant place, with a great view of the plains
and thickets below, and decent rocks to sit on, often offering good views of animals and
occasionally revealing animals that might warrant closer inspection if the conditions
are right. I have done many walks in that area and do not recall a single one when we
haven't had the 'coffee break' by the lone tree at the end of the spur.

But back to Eugene's walk. As soon as they reached the hill they got lucky. On the
northern side at the foot was a moderately large group of buffalo slowly moving away to
drink at a nearby dam. The sun was behind the walking group, so it was a particularly
good sighting from a very safe, elevated location.

Suddenly their idyll was disturbed by the sound of branches breaking and loud
trumpeting. Elephants! Coming their way too. They were downwind of the elephants
which was good, and they hoped that with any sort of luck the animals would take the
path that runs around the southern side of Euphorbia Hill, frequently used by all sorts
of game and safely out of sight. Nevertheless, ever cautious, they moved the guests to
the slightly lower north-east corner of the hill, where there was a bit more cover. And
they waited. Sure enough, a breeding herd of some 30–40 or more elephants behaved
as predicted, and passed them by, moving unusually quickly and a bit noisily as if on a
mission. The noise spooked the buffalo group below who ran off, crashing through the
bushes at high speed.

Sometimes there are 'tail-end Charlies' following a breeding herd. These are usually
single young bulls who have been ejected from the herd because of their age but who

hang around a little way back for a year or more. A bit like teenagers in human families. With that in mind Eugene moved cautiously up the short distance to the fairly open crown of the hill to check. It was worth doing. Another dozen or so elephants, 60–70 metres away, were marching steadily in his direction, clearly intending to traverse the hill instead of circumnavigating it. This was more of a problem. He gestured to Shaun to move the clients down the steeper side of the hill, out of the elephants' line of fire so to speak, and he began a careful tactical withdrawal to join them.

That was the moment when everything kicked off. A very large female, possibly the matriarch of this group, saw some movement from the guest party and began to run towards them, though not at full tilt. Her ears were extended, she was making a lot of noise and swinging her trunk about, generally the sort of picture that suggested she might stop. Shaun turned his group and faced the charge. He chambered a round, shouted at the elephant in quite extraordinarily profane language, and took aim as she approached. She stopped literally 2 metres away from him, which meant that he was aiming up her brain at about a 45-degree angle. Eugene heard him repeating to his guests, 'Stand still. Do not run.' He'd played things by the book and the threat was now more under control. During all this Eugene had moved so that he was standing at right angles to the cow. He, too, had chambered a round after Shaun who was now, in effect, the trail leader and was in a decent position for a brain shot. If he was to shoot, then Eugene would shoot too. That's the accepted procedure. So it was a stand-off. And they waited to see if she would just turn and walk away which, at that time, seemed the likely resolution.

Eugene's confrontation with the elephant on Euphorbia Hill

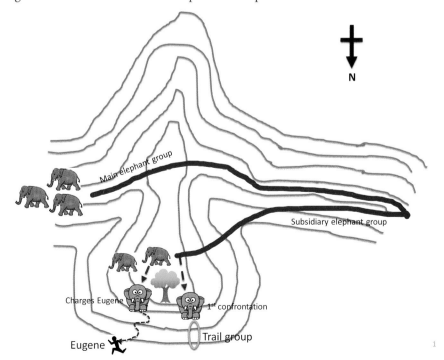

Suddenly Shaun shouted, 'Watch out, Eugene, there's another one coming at you.' Eugene looked left and there was a young cow approaching at high speed. Her behaviour was very different. Her ears were flattened, trunk tucked up, and not a sound did she utter. But even as he watched with horrid fascination he could see that she wasn't actually coming directly towards him. On glancing right he realised with a chill of horror, the blood-freezing kind, that one of the guests, a young lady, had felt she would be safer where he was and was running towards him. Shouting 'Stand still!' had no effect whatsoever. Instinctively he moved towards her and grabbed her. By then the elephant was on them so he pushed the girl hard, so hard in fact that she went flying. This action meant the rifle was now in his left, and wrong, hand. He hit the elephant with it just the same. There was only one thing to do now and he did it: he ran like hell steeply down the hill, instinctively away from the guests. Even now Eugene clearly remembers the path he ran down, aiming for a tree trunk lying on its side that might provide some cover. A glance over his shoulder confirmed the elephant was still there, though all he could see was an ear and the trunk that she tried to put around his left side. He punched the trunk and tried to turn round quickly to try a desperate random shot. But at that moment she ran her tusk through his shorts and down along his leg, amazingly without breaking the skin. With this as leverage she then simply scooped him up and threw him through the air.

The rifle went goodness knows where. All he recalls of the next few moments is dust and legs. The elephant was kicking him, kicking him, and he was rolling over and over between her legs trying to keep out of the way. At one point he managed to get onto his hands and knees to try and get up to run again, but she gave him a hefty crack with her trunk and he was propelled through the air again, this time landing on his back. When he looked up, there she was, directly above. Slowly she lowered her head. This was it, the end. No life flashed before his eyes, just disbelief that this could be happening. But suddenly she just stood up straight, shook her head and slowly jogged away into the bushes, tail erect as it is when an elephant is angry or feels threatened. (Later he learned that this was probably at exactly the same time as the matriarch had pushed off. Maybe they had communicated.)

As soon as it became clear that the elephant was moving away Eugene's first thought was 'Where's my rifle? I must find my rifle.' After all, he thought, she might decide to pop back for a bit more fun. Shaun called asking if he was OK. 'Fine,' he replied. 'Get the guests back to the vehicle.' But he still couldn't find the rifle. He walked around searching for it, probably in a trance-like state, and he doesn't recall any pain at that stage, presumably still pumping adrenaline. He even found and picked up a lens from some spectacles, later returning it to its owner, the guest who he'd shoved so violently.

Then, quite close, he heard more noise of breaking branches. 'Here we go again,' he thought, but it was just Shaun, exercising his off-road driving skills in an effort to locate him. 'Let's go back to the lodge,' he suggested. 'Forget the rifle; we can deal with that later.'

Eugene struggled to get into the passenger seat and everything began to hurt: his neck, his wrist and one hand. His face was swollen, and he was bleeding from somewhere though the source was not apparent. At this point he began to feel quite damaged. But his legs were fine and he could move his feet which was a great relief. After receiving some basic first aid at the lodge he was transferred to a local hospital where – miraculously he thought – they found no fractures and no serious internal injuries. He was back at home with his girlfriend later the same day.

That's not the end of the story. He still had what had now become an obsession about the rifle, and so later on the day of the incident a guide colleague went to the spot and, not only could he not locate the rifle, but didn't even find the path down which Eugene had hurtled trying to escape. Eugene decided that the man must be an idiot. The path was blindingly obvious and the rifle was somewhere on it or close to it. He would have to go himself. So a few days later out he went with a couple of scouts from the Parks Board and the same idiot. Eugene was very nervous, and any sound in the bush put him on edge. There was indeed no path. He couldn't believe it. That wasn't possible. But the scouts clearly identified the zig-zag course he had taken. He couldn't believe that either: surely he'd run in a straight line. The elephant's spoor following his trail was the clincher, and close to the end of the signs of his flight they found the rifle, cleanly snapped into two pieces.

It took a long time for Eugene to recover properly from the incident. Because he knew he was a tough guy (and he is) he started leading walks again quite quickly. But even though he'd been a walking guide for 18 years, every walk now was like the first of his career, with anxiety at every turn. Every day became a struggle. Eventually he heeded all the sensible suggestions that came his way, notably from his girlfriend (now wife) and the lodge manager, and sought professional help, which was highly successful. Afterwards, one evening he drove himself out into the bush and parked in the midst of a large breeding herd of elephants, throwing the vehicle keys into the back seat to resist the temptation of driving off if they approached too close. Then he closed his eyes and listened to their movements, their eating sounds, their communication. And all was well.

One thing that this epic account confirms is the importance of, and one of the problems with, the so-called 'pre-trail briefing' which all guides deliver to their guests before setting foot in the wilderness. There is a fairly long list of do's and don'ts, but the crucially important item is what to do in an emergency. The default instructions are straightforward enough: 'Stay close behind me' and 'DO NOT RUN.' It is usual to add that should the guide vary this the guest must obey exactly, immediately and without question. In Eugene's scary story the guest either hadn't listened, didn't remember or, most likely, had panicked. Repetition from time to time might help, but then those on the receiving end of the further exhortation may be made to feel like naughty schoolchildren. It's an interesting issue. Finally, Eugene would be the first to admit that he's a big guy, and he suggested to me that maybe the lady concerned simply felt that he offered a better opportunity for decent cover.

Spare a thought whilst reading these stories to consider why these wonderful, almost legendary, wild creatures should at times act so aggressively when meeting humans on foot. After all, we are just walking as a group with guides whose ethos is a

The author briefing some particularly tough-looking apprentice guides at Limpopo Guiding Academy. A comprehensive briefing is vital before any walk in a dangerous game area. *(Mark Stavrakis)*

commitment to the enjoyment and protection of nature. The answer is that surely this is the animal's turf, not ours. They react to perceived threats to themselves and their offspring just as we humans do. By flight or by fight.

Respect the bush or trouble will surely follow.

5 RHINOCEROS

Do you know what a rhinoceros looks like?
Of course. It's a big, ugly animal.

Eugène Ionesco *Rhinoceros* (1959)

Game drives are rarely dangerous. Dismounting from the vehicle and hoofing it into the bush, on whatever errand, may be. This was the circumstance that befell Themba Zwane when he was working as a tracker at a lodge in the Greater Kruger. He and his guide, in a game drive vehicle with guests, had been assiduously following the tracks of a very large black rhino through quite thick terrain of rocky areas with a mixed bag of bushes, studded with fig trees. There were few better local areas to find black rhino. After 15 minutes or so the tracks disappeared into off-road thicker bush and, when they had driven a full circuit, they did not see them emerge. Clearly, the animal had remained within the block.

Themba's task was to proceed on foot to try and locate the animal so that the guests could have their first sight of this magnificent creature. The procedure is called 'trailing'. Whilst he was doing this the guide would entertain the guests not too far away and keep in contact with Themba by radio.

Following the tracks was initially quite easy but all too soon the rhino had passed over rockier ground and they became much trickier to follow. Themba's pace slowed. Here and there were the tiniest traces of the animal's progress: a scuff in the sand, a tiny flattened area of grass, a partial footprint. These, coupled with his intuition as to which route the rhino was likely to take, led him unerringly back onto a clearer trail. Until now he had, from time to time, heard sounds of the rhino's progress. Noisy feeding, some heavy footfall and the classic calls of oxpeckers seeking their own sustenance on the rhino's back were all there. Then suddenly there was silence. He stopped and listened. Not a sound. Almost certainly the rhino had lain down and might even be sleeping. The day was rapidly heating up and it was very likely that the animal would try and locate suitable shade for a snooze. So Themba decided correctly to slow his pace a little and ensure that he didn't lose the track. Later he told

[Left] Spoor of a large, male white rhinoceros being trailed by a group of guides. *(Brett Horley)*

[Right] Hot on the trail of the white rhino. *(Brett Horley)*

me that he thought that focusing on the track was probably his undoing for when he suddenly looked up there was the rhino, now looking enormous, about 10 metres directly in front and looking at him. A bad moment. The rhino snorted loudly and began to stamp on the ground. Quickly he considered his options. Stand his ground or flee? Then the animal charged, Themba shouted, but the rhino didn't falter and its speed increased. So Themba ran. Ran as if his life depended on it, which it probably did. The rhino was quickly catching him up, but there was a tree just ahead. Themba leapt into it and started to climb. He could, as he said, 'feel the rhino's hot breath from its nostrils right on my bum'. As he was climbing the rhino was stretching its head up and trying to hook him with its horns. He reached safety, unless this was a new and not hitherto described species of climbing rhinoceros.

After 30 seconds the animal gave up and ran away. Themba climbed down, sat on the ground and began to laugh. The laughter of hysterical relief that continued as he gazed with amazement at the tree that had been his refuge. How could he possibly have climbed it? Later, when the guide and guests returned in the vehicle having been summoned by radio, they explored the area to try and rediscover the rhino. They succeeded quite quickly, only for the animal to charge the vehicle. He was either ill, wounded or simply very troubled by the sudden appearance of humans.

Most of the alarming rhinoceros stories arising from walking in the bush involve black rhinos, and speculative reasons for this emerge in other parts of this book.

However, it's important not to dismiss white rhinos from anyone's dangerous animal list. Their habit of grazing in open areas usually makes them easy to see and often they make for a straightforward approach. But at the end of the day they are a very large animal, and the males up to 1,000 kilograms heavier than their black counterparts – indeed, twice as heavy – move much more speedily than might be expected, and like all other animals dislike being surprised. So generally speaking if it's at all possible it's a good idea to avoid surprising one when walking in the bush.

It was a lovely summer's day, a light breeze just disturbing the trees, when Sophia Lehr, a walking guide, her tracker Lucky and their guest Peter set out for a walk. Bush walks are never routine and surprises never off the radar of a competent guide, but this outing started calmly enough. There was interest galore. First the track of a slender mongoose and its scat almost immediately followed by the accidental flushing from cover of a female honey badger. They followed her covertly to the burrow where there was a single cub and watched the interaction between mother and child without being seen as they withdrew. That was a rare sighting, and a pretty special one. Soon they passed a hyaena den, but no-one was at home: as is typical with spotted hyaenas, the clan had made one of their irregular and unpredictable house moves. Later giraffe and zebra made brief guest appearances but didn't linger.

The slender tree climbed by Themba to escape the rhino's wrath.
(*Themba Zwane*)

All too quickly it was time for the party to make their way back towards the lodge. Here they were in open country with good visibility and the small group passed close to a gully of a now dry stream, about 1.5 metres deep and 2 metres wide and partially shaded by guarri bushes growing along the flat ground of the rim. At this point Sophia suddenly espied the spine of a white rhino, just visible above the lip of the gully and only a short distance ahead. As the wind was unfavourable and likely to alert the rhino to their presence she quickly ushered the group away from the gully edge and quietly past the animal. The plan was straightforward. It would be good, she thought, to get a better view of the rhino by crossing the gully where that was possible and viewing the rhino from the opposite bank. Ahead she could see a likely crossing point. It was steep-sided but feasible. That's when the trouble started. The rhino, now seen with a sub-adult

Southern white rhino with classic square-lipped appearance. The front horn is remarkably long. The anterior (front) horn is remarkably long in this particular animal. *(Patricia Goodwin)*

offspring in attendance, reached the crossing point at precisely the same moment as Sophia, and against all expectations climbed up the steep gully side with impressive agility. They were only a few metres apart and, the wind coming from directly behind the walking group, the humans were quickly identified by the animal. The cow shuffled a few steps forward. snout to the ground. She was very close now, but impeded by a small log on the ground on which she bumped her nose. But she seemed unsure of what to do, shuffling her feet a bit more but never appearing aggressive. Sophia was standing very still with her tracker and the guest right up close behind her.

This standoff seemed to last for hours. Sophia didn't chamber a round and had decided right from the beginning that there was no way she was going to shoot such a beautiful and precious animal. She slapped the magazine of the rifle and made as much noise as possible in an effort to dissuade the rhino from aggressive action. Indeed, there was no charge, but the animal did take a couple of steps towards her. Clearly it had every intention of leaving the gully even though the three walkers were in her way. 'Jump left!' shouted Sophia, and they all did. It was like a rehearsed synchronised dance move. At the same moment the rhino and calf jogged up and out of the gully diagonally away from them and lumbered off into some trees and out of sight.

Sophia held an immediate debrief to ensure that everyone was OK and uninjured, as well as quickly discussing what had happened and why she took what turned out to be the highly professional and successful action that she had. And they walked back to the lodge.

The aftermath is fascinating, and highlights how individual participants react so differently from each other, all depending on their experience and whether they had to make very fast executive decisions. That evening Peter, the guest, was in Sophia's words 'amazing' both in his behaviour at the time of the incident and his subsequent reaction of saying how much he had enjoyed the entire experience. Lucky, the tracker, was also in fine form, excited and laughing about the whole thing. At that point so was Sophia.

The next two days were exceedingly busy at the lodge, too busy for any serious reflection. But then later in the evening when the lodge had quietened down, quite out of the blue, she suddenly felt a buzzing throughout her body as if she was electrified and an inability to sleep. In some ways it was as if she was taking drugs of some kind. Fortunately this all subsided quickly and by morning all was well. Almost certainly this represented the well-known 'delayed shock' or, in some people's eyes, a very mild version of post-traumatic stress.

Sophia has always regarded this incident as a great learning experience. Something, she believes, that all guides would benefit from so that they can know for sure how they might respond in any future, possibly more threatening or dangerous, situation. It's also interesting to note that in many of the stories in this compilation, other guides reported highly significant post-incident symptoms even though the nature of these varied from person to person.

In some quarters white rhinos have a very benign reputation. This isn't appropriate. Sure, they tend to be easy to approach for a whole variety of reasons, but should never be regarded as always benign of attitude especially if they have young in attendance. Even if they haven't, in the wild you can't just stroll up and pat them on the nose. Being hit by an animal weighing around 1,700 kilograms is dangerous to health even without the potential damage from two pointy horns.

6 MORE ELEPHANT MOMENTS

It will come as no surprise to guides that the animal most frequently appearing in potentially dangerous and even fatal incidents when on foot in the bush is *Loxodonta africana*, that sometimes not-too-gentle giant of the bush, loved by most and admired by all, the African elephant.

My own first significant 'elephant moment' was a fair time ago when I was a tourist, informed only by tourist experiences, heading for a camp on the Kwando river in northern Botswana. We'd been collected from the airstrip by a guide and tracker in a game drive vehicle and were making our leisurely way to a scented flannel and the customary welcome soft drink at the lodge, stopping from time to time, as is the custom, to gaze at things of interest. Suddenly, rounding a bend we saw, maybe 150 metres in front of us, a large group of elephants, including several obvious youngsters, very much about their own business but camped fairly and squarely astride the track on which we were travelling. Now I wouldn't claim that the guide exactly gunned the engine but he certainly didn't slacken speed either. With hindsight the results were entirely predictable. One extremely large female was clearly unimpressed with the suddenness and speed of our approach and without any hesitation put her head down, flattened her ears and charged, silently, which in its own way was more unnerving than high-volume trumpeting. Two other females joined the party immediately behind her and we were instantly faced with what I thought, even in my bush innocence, might be something of a crisis. It seemed the guide thought so too, for we came to a dramatic stop in a cloud of dust. He shouted at the elephants. The tracker, sitting on that little rather exposed seat on the front left-hand side of the vehicle, shouted at the guide. I speak no Setswana but the gist was clear. The sisterhood just kept on coming, still silent and gathering momentum. We were halfway through the turn when the ladies arrived within trunk-striking range of the tracker's seat, its recent occupant making a very determined though precarious bid back across the bonnet of the vehicle for what he perceived as the safety of the front passenger seat. We got away by the skin of our teeth, though the elephants chased us for at least another 50 metres before giving up. When we'd all calmed down our guide told us with considerable surprise in his still shaky voice that the local elephants were usually so placid you could just drive through them.

This was my first important and never-to-be-forgotten bush lesson. All animals are unpredictable, and how they behaved yesterday may have no correlation whatsoever with how they behave today. Actually, the only predictable thing is their unpredictability. Elephants are well-established members of this club and, as well as being the size of a small house, have a wide variety of weapons systems at their disposal to really spoil your day if things go awfully wrong. Personally, when on foot in the bush I'm more wary of breeding herds of elephants than any other animals, and I know many guides who share that view.

However many times I've been walking in the bush I still find it perfectly extraordinary that an animal as absolutely huge as an elephant can be so difficult to spot even when it's only in half-decent cover. Even then, sometimes all you see is a sort of bouldery shadow behind green curtains of foliage. Is it actually a boulder? And if it's an elephant, which bit am I seeing and which way is it facing? Also, their cushioned feet give them an extraordinary, almost mystical, ability to move soundlessly through the bush. First-time visitors look frankly disbelieving when I tell them of the time I was digging a fire pit at a camp-out in Botswana and I had to be alerted by a guide colleague that a decent-sized bull elephant had approached within 40 metres behind me across an open plain without me hearing anything. Fortunately my colleague was the one with focus on the surroundings (and the rifle), and the elephant wasn't the slightest bit interested in me, just ambling past to get at some particularly tender leaves on the trees which provided shade for our tents.

Elcke and Shaun Malan manage and guide at a most delightful camp on the Khwai river in Botswana. They looked after me with great kindness and efficiency when I was doing some training there some time ago. Whilst I was there they recorded for me an event which occurred whilst they were managing a camp in Tanzania some years before. All accounts of serious confrontations with elephants are intense, but this represents one of the most dramatic tales of any animal confrontation and its aftermath I have ever heard. This re-telling of the story was such an emotional experience for both Elcke and Shaun – though even more so for the two listeners – that I have retained the original account more or less verbatim. Elcke sets out the background and starts the tale.

Elcke

I remember the afternoon vividly. It had started so happily too. I'd been playing with our daughter Nala by the swimming pool in the camp where Shaun and I were managers. Nala, almost one year old, was splashing her feet and laughing so much that it was such a joy to be with her. Then our assistant manager Simon arrived poolside. Simon was Maasai. He was behaving oddly, shuffling a bit, avoiding eye contact – you know how it is when someone has something difficult to tell you but doesn't know how to start.'

'Simon,' I said, 'do you want to tell me something'?'

'There's something wrong with the radio.'

'What's wrong with the radio?'

'No, no. Something on the walk. They found the girl.'

'Simon, I don't understand. What do you mean?'

Apparently John, our game drive vehicle driver, had radioed to say that they had found a young woman at the side of a track in the bush, the same young woman that Shaun, my husband and the head guide at the camp, had taken on a bush walk earlier in the day. She had, it seemed, just walked out of the bush onto the track close to the vehicle and was covered in blood.

'Whose blood is it?'

'It's not her blood.'

'Whose blood is it?'

'It's Shaun's blood.'

'Is Shaun there?'

'No, they can't find him.'

This was really scary, and I wasn't getting any real picture of what was going on. So, leaving Nala with our nanny, I hurried off to the camp office and the radio to speak to John the driver and Kibori the tracker, who was also on the vehicle. Simon would need to translate the conversation into and from Swahili. This made the dialogue halting, somewhat monosyllabic and very difficult.

'John, are you with the girl now?'

'Yes.'

'Is she OK?'

'Yes.'

'Is Shaun there?'

'No, he's not.'

'What's happened?'

'All she can say is that it was an elephant.'

'Is Shaun alive?'

'I don't know. She doesn't know. She's covered with blood but it's not hers.'

'John, tell Kibori to start tracking. Find Shaun – find my husband. Does she know where he is? How far away is he?'

'She doesn't know where she came from. We'll go and try to find him.'

The next 10–15 minutes passed very slowly. It was like an eternity. So many thoughts raced through my mind. Was Shaun dead? If he was severely injured what must I do? Who should I contact? What about Nala? What about the guests in the camp? And still waiting, waiting.

At times like these you have to occupy your mind and there were so many things to do. So I cleared an area near the lodge gate and we assembled blankets, a stretcher and all the first aid kit that we had. I had contacted the camp owners with an outline of the problem, and they assured me they were standing by but would need further information before arranging a medevac by aircraft. Amazingly, soon afterwards I began to receive phone calls from everyone and everywhere. Doctors in Arusha asking if we had more information, the medevac people wanting health insurance and passport numbers, other lodges asking how things were going. The bush telegraph – in reality these days the mobile phone network – was working at full speed. Also I was anxious to keep Nala out of the way. She mustn't see her daddy covered in blood or perhaps dead, so I sent one of our guys up to ensure the nanny stayed in our house with her.

'Kibori, have you found him? Kibori, do you have him?'

The answer was always, 'No, no, no.'

But suddenly the radio burst into life again. 'We've got him!'

'Is he alive?'

'Yes he's alive, but he's bleeding to death. There's so much blood. We're bringing him back to camp.'

I don't know how long it took. Maybe 20 minutes. It seemed like a lifetime. But finally the vehicle arrived. Shaun was conscious but quite confused: he even tried to get out of the car unassisted. He was very bashed about, his face was scratched and there was blood everywhere, but my husband was alive. And as I made him lie down his first words to me were 'I love you'.

SHAUN

For the first hour the walk was deceptively straightforward. It was around three in the afternoon when we'd headed out and I'd planned a route I knew well. There was just a young female guest, on her first visit to the bush, and me. I guess she was in her late twenties or early thirties. The idea was to walk for a couple of hours, meet the game drive vehicle at a pre-arranged spot and enjoy the traditional sundowner drinks at a suitably pleasant location.

We arrived at a wide and dry riverbed. The country was fairly open there, though there were isolated trees along the banks and a few clumps of bushes. I looked around but didn't see anything of note and we started across. Just over halfway suddenly, to my left and about 25 metres away, a very small elephant calf appeared and started to scream as soon as it saw us. Right behind came Mum, very fast and with serious intent, ears flat and head lowered. By this time we were close to a massive sycamore fig, just a few metres ahead. My thought was to get both of us behind this and out of sight: maybe that would do the trick.

But the elephant came straight on so I shouted to the girl to run up the small bank behind us and make for a large acacia about 100 metres away. She ran and I turned, chambering a round as I did so, but no sooner had I closed the bolt than the elephant was on me, hitting me hard in the chest with her forehead. I went down flat on my back like a ton of bricks, with her head still pressing on my chest. She raised her head a little and started to press down, still on my chest, with her trunk. Laughably in hindsight, I tried to hold the trunk off me – I remember vividly a close-up view of all the wrinkles. Then quickly she flipped me over with it and immediately I felt a massive blow from a tusk in my backside. The ivory went all the way down from my bum into my thigh. I don't remember any pain. That came later. It was just a huge blow. She flipped me over onto my back again and, this time using the other tusk, pierced my knee. As a finale she

Peaceful photograph of typically very protective mother.
Sometimes they are not so peaceful … *(Maryann Williams)*

began to kick me around like a football. By this time I felt as though I was in a washing machine, rolling around with each kick, waiting for the end.

Suddenly she stopped and walked away. Just like that. Somehow I managed to get up and headed, staggering, towards the acacia. I had no rifle and no idea where it was. But I remember that I was laughing out loud, which is very strange. Relief at realising I was alive I guess. I quickly recognised that I was losing a lot of blood but kept going, shouting to the girl to get up into the tree out of sight just in case the elephant returned. When I joined her I climbed into a low fork and wedged my buttocks against a branch to try and reduce the blood loss. It was still an hour to pick-up time and I had no way of communicating with the lodge. After about 30 minutes I began to pass out, and understandably the young lady wanted to go and try to find help. It was the only sensible thing to do notwithstanding the attendant risk. So I pointed out the direction, about a kilometre to the road, I reckoned with intervening ground that fortunately was quite open and thus a bit safer. She was very brave and set out after helping me to the ground. By this time I couldn't stand and felt worse and worse and weaker and weaker with every passing minute. The centre of my chest was very painful and I was struggling to breathe. I lay on the ground looking at the grass in front of my eyes. I was too weak even to lift my head and just lay there, praying that someone would come soon. I couldn't imagine how I'd even reached the tree – it must have been endorphins or adrenaline or whatever. It was a hard time. It seemed to be hours and I felt so alone, so very alone.

'My chest, my chest,' Shaun kept repeating. His chest did appear to be expanding normally but his breathing was very erratic. There was blood everywhere. When we turned him to examine his back, half of his buttock fell open like a flap and I could see all the inside of his upper leg and bottom.

'Is it bad?' he asked.

'No, no, it's looking good. Don't worry.'

We taped him up, which seemed to stop most of the bleeding leaving just a bit of an ooze. Then I sought and received more medical advice on the phone, impressing everyone how vital it was to get him to a hospital as soon as possible. But there were problems. The nearest airstrip was in the park two hours away, and by now it was too late and too dark for it to be useful. The medevac helicopter could get to us, I was told, but couldn't take off again in the dark. It was clear that we would have to set out by road and, hopefully, meet the paramedics en route.

'Simon, you take care of all the guests. Explain there's been a problem but not too many details. Look after the girl who was with Shaun.' 'Get the bakkie (pick-up) and a mattress for the back, get our passports and an overnight bag.'

I organised another vehicle to travel behind us, with John as driver, Nala and the nanny. They had instructions not to come close particularly if we had to stop for medical reasons but just keep us in good sight. David would drive us, I'd be in the back with Shaun; and Kibori, our tracker who steadfastly refused to leave Shaun's side, would also come with us.

We set off. On a good day it took three hours to reach the main road. Now it was night, and a tricky drive with animals all around and wandering onto the track. It was all very scary. Shaun started to pass out from time to time and then he wouldn't answer me. Actually at one point I was so panicky that I smacked him hard in the face to make him speak. It was taking so long. We reached a T-junction after three hours so I knew there was another hour to go. Then we had a puncture. That could have tipped me over completely but David changed the wheel faster than he had ever done it before. I swear it took less than three minutes. Everyone got out except Shaun of course, and it was almost like watching an F1 team in the pits. As we continued Shaun became more and more agitated, which I thought might be lack of oxygen.

'We're going too fast and it's making me worse.' So we would slow down.

'It's too bumpy, you must go faster. I'm going to die, I know I am.' We couldn't get it right for him.

At last we reached the road and the ambulance. I was so relieved. It's over. I can hand him over. Now we'll be OK. The medics put him in the ambulance and gave him oxygen. Good. Then they put a dressing on a tiny scratch on his head but didn't examine him. They just looked, said 'Eesh' and gravely shook their heads. I was dumbstruck. They weren't going to do anything in the way of further treatment. I don't know what I expected, but surely they could do something. So the anxiety didn't really begin to settle until we reached the hospital in Arusha. Even there they did very little apart from give him morphine and keep him in an area they called their Intensive Care Unit though it wasn't like any ICU I'd ever seen before. There was little or no investigation. After three very difficult days for us the company who owned our lodge agreed that he needed to be transferred to a bigger hospital, in Nairobi in Kenya. So they flew him there whilst Nala and I went by road and got there first. This was the Aga Khan University Hospital, and the care was fantastic. Immediate assessment on arrival, in theatre within 45 minutes and, after ten days as an in-patient, a recuperative stay in a nearby hotel. As a memento of his stay a member of the surgical team presented him with a small piece of ivory, part of the tusk that had done the damage, retrieved from the wound somewhere near his knee.

✳✳✳

Of course that wasn't the end. He needed crutches to walk for two months, and it was a good six months before he was physically back to normal. It needed a while for the confidence to return but it wasn't long after that before he was guiding on foot again.

Shaun says that although he was quite wary at first he was soon back to how he had felt before the incident, with one important difference. Now he had a lot more respect for elephants and indeed admired them all the more. Even with the benefit of hindsight, if he had to do that walk again he would do it the same. He wasn't approaching the elephant. She just appeared and came at him. Should he just have shot her immediately the charge started? 'That's a difficult call,' he said. 'You always try not to shoot an animal and get out of the way. It's just that on that occasion it didn't work out.' He still wears a necklace that sports as a centre-piece the piece of elephant ivory taken out of his buttock during surgery.

And what happened to the lady guest? She, and her mother who was also staying in the camp, had support and counselling from the caretaker managers who arrived on the same evening that Elcke left with Shaun. They had seemed to be in good enough spirits before leaving the camp,

Shaun Malan wearing the necklace with its integral part, the piece of elephant tusk removed from somewhere near his knee. *(Patricia Goodwin)*

The formidable weaponry of a large elephant is evident here. Forehead, trunk, tusks and feet may all be used with devastating effects. *(Patricia Goodwin)*

and subsequently wrote to Shaun saying how pleased they were that he was well on the road to recovery. Indeed the young lady said that, after all, the episode had given her the 'best summer holiday story ever'!

When you consider the huge size and power of an adult elephant, females often weighing more than 3,000 kilograms and males anything up to 6,000 kilograms or more, standing up to 4 metres at shoulder height, it's easy to understand that it requires very little effort for them to inflict grievous damage to a human. The trunk, an embryonic fusion of upper lip and nose, and a largely muscular structure, is a fascinating component of its weaponry. We often speak about its functionality in grasping, twisting, pulling and touching plus its importance in breathing, smelling, communication and even as a snorkel. Less often do we underline its rôle in defence or attack. But at 2 metres or more in length and weighing up to 180 kilograms it's a fearsome bit of kit, and you really don't want to get whacked by it.

'If you listen, the bush will tell you what you need to hear.' Sometimes this old bush phrase will come to your rescue when other senses have failed to pick up that vital clue, and will rescue you from at best embarrassment and at worst disaster. This is why experienced guides stop very frequently, looking for all the world as if they're a bit lost and are wondering which way to go. But sometimes there are no clues and little or no warning. The previous elephant stories fell comfortably into that category, but the next, related very frankly and with laudable insight, examines and exemplifies a slightly different potential problem for guides.

Brett Horley is a friend who has been guiding more or less since he left school. During that time he has earned a fantastic reputation not just as a field guide at the top of his game but also as a great organiser of safari trips with his own company. For me there is also another side to his character which particularly appeals. Apart from keeping very up to date on all things to do with the bush, Brett is extremely keen on scientific evidence to underpin his guiding and has that self-awareness that good guides, good doctors and good pilots, amongst other professionals, all possess. He told me this story, which occurred many years ago, in the spirit of others learning from an incident which befell him at an early stage of his career.

> Just in case you thought elephants were all sweetness, I can attest to the fact that this one had the time of her life scaring the bejeezus out of those dudes.
>
> - James Patterson. American novelist (b. 1947)

It happened when Brett was leading a walking safari in the Klaserie Nature Reserve with four guests: an elderly American couple, a young Dutch guy and a professional photographer from Norway. Brett's colleague and back-up for the occasion was Isaac 'Eyes' Nkuna. 'Eyes' was a Shangaan and real man of the bush who had grown up herding goats inside and outside the park boundaries. He'd earned his nickname from his uncanny ability to spot absolutely anything and everything that moved out there. He was an unbelievably good tracker and could read the bush like no one Brett had ever seen before. I too have walked with Eyes, and his talents are awesome. Tracking lions is his speciality act, and he follows their likely path through the bush as if he were a lion himself: that's the trick of course, being able to imagine that you are the animal.

On the final morning of a four-night trail they did a two-hour walk in and along the banks of a large dry riverbed, a tributary of the Klaserie river. It's a beautiful place to walk; big trees and rocky outcrops that make a great habitat for leopards and old buffalo bulls. Only a few months before Brett had watched a leopard kill a duiker on a walk in this area.

As the group neared the end of the walk they heard the cracking sound of elephants breaking branches. It's a great advantage to hear them from a distance, as it allows a nice, slow, careful approach. So they climbed out of the riverbed and used the elevated northern side to look south towards the breeding herd. Here there was a kopje, a small rocky outcrop, and from the top they watched the elephants in the distance, pulling down branches, kicking up attractive vegetation on the ground, stripping a bit of bark, all the things that elephants do when feeding. The wind was in the group's favour; they had height advantage, and the riverbed was between them and the elephants, so the animals had no idea of people being anywhere near them. Everybody found a comfortable seat, relaxed and enjoyed the moment, watching the family below mingling, rumbling, feeding and playing. It seemed to be the perfect end to four days in the bush: a beautiful Lowveld morning, the rocks warming up under the sun's rays, a classic and timeless African bush scene below them as they reminisced about their time in the wilderness. And all the while the elephants fed peacefully below.

By this time it was getting quite late in the morning so the two guides decided that Eyes would head back alone to the vehicle, which they'd left in the bush where they had started the walk. That way the guests could enjoy the sighting and the solitude for another 15 minutes or so. Then they would use the radio and arrange to meet up at a pre-arranged rendezvous (RV) in about half an hour. So off he went. The group sat a little longer, watching the elephants slowly moving away, had a drink of water and then continued in their original direction to meet Eyes.

After they came down off the kopje they continued along the bank of the riverbed, the elephants having moved off into the distance on the opposite bank. Not long afterwards Brett could hear the vehicle heading towards the RV so he radioed Isaac and confirmed that they would be with him in about five minutes. In hindsight, Brett believes that it was at that point that his thoughts drifted, thinking about the next trail he would be starting that afternoon, winning the lottery, or something equally dreamy – and, it must be said, potentially distracting. They strolled along in companionable silence and entered a large area where high sodium levels in the soil had prevented trees, grasses and bushes from establishing, leaving it bare and open. A sodic area would be the correct term. Guides slow down and take particular care through open areas like that, and Brett remembers slowly scanning from right to left. As his neck turned the last few degrees he saw an elephant cow. Her ears were stretched out. and on either side, right up against her legs, were two calves of different ages. She was coming straight towards them!

She was reasonably far away – was this really going to be a problem? But almost at the same instant, just about the time he saw the elephants, the radio on his belt crackled into life 'Horley, do you see the ndlopfu? Horley, ndlopfu!' Isaac was calling urgently across the airwaves. ('Ndlopfu' is Shangaan for 'elephant'.)

With this warning from Isaac, Brett's brain went from being totally at ease into critical mode. Time was compressed. Probably it all took less than a second. He still says that the image of that elephant mother with her calves almost attached to her will never leave his mind. She was trumpeting and coming directly towards them, covering another 50 metres very quickly, though there was still sufficient time for him and his party to react sensibly. They had inadvertently come directly between her, with her children, and the rest of their family unit, even though the others were almost a kilometre away.

Brett shouted to the guests, 'Run to the river bed and go down.' Of course, he'd told them on the first day that rule number one was 'Don't run'. But because of his tone of voice and what they could see in front they all hit the burners and did exactly what he said. Then he screamed and swore at the elephant, and whistled loudly and aggressively – but she just kept coming. He turned around and also raced towards the edge of the riverbank. At high speed he opened the bolt of the rifle and didn't close it again. With hindsight, Brett said that his thinking was, 'I'll open it halfway so if I need to shoot all I have to do is close the bolt and squeeze the trigger. And it will eliminate the possibility of an inadvertent discharge.'

At the moment he turned around towards the river he couldn't see any of the guests but presumed that they'd simply hopped down into the riverbed. So when he got to the edge he simply jumped straight off. It was a six-foot drop down onto the sand. This was perfect. The elephant wouldn't be able to follow him. He fell, face planted into the sand, arms and legs flailing. When he looked up he saw that the four guests were still racing straight down the drainage line away from him. This was not the plan. 'Stop!' he shouted. 'Come back here, come back to me!' When he'd told them 'run to the riverbed and go down', he'd simply meant they should get down the bank into the sand and squat down. But in that situation it had been too easy to interpret it as 'go down the riverbed'!

By now the female elephant had reached the bank above Brett and was screaming and trumpeting. The rest of the 20 + family unit had obviously been alerted to the extreme stress of a relative and they were charging about in panic. They had encountered Isaac in the vehicle and were chasing him around the bush: he was shouting on the radio to try and get an answer from Brett, who could hear alarmingly loud elephant noise in the background, almost drowning Isaac's voice. There was noise everywhere. But Brett couldn't spare a hand or a moment to get a message to him as his elephant was now planning a route down into the drainage line. Things were not looking good.

Elephants are much more agile and nimble than they appear. They are good climbers but don't descend steep ground at all well and have to negotiate any such slope quite slowly. The situation was that now the guests were running back towards Brett, though hampered by the deep, soft river sand. At the same time the female elephant was directly above them, running in the opposite direction, trying to find a route down into the riverbed. In other circumstances, filmed, this would have appeared wildly funny but it was at that precise moment that Brett understood that this elephant really was after them. She clearly had seriously aggressive intentions, and the noise, stress and panic were getting to everyone.

By now the guests were closing in on Brett – so what next? Unhappily, unlike the relatively low bank that they had jumped down, the opposite bank was essentially 30 feet of vertical sand and rock. But he'd run out of options. 'Climb the cliff, climb the cliff!' he yelled. When he looked round he saw that the elephant had reached the riverbed and had, it seemed to him, acquired her target. Him. Indeed, locked on to it. He raised the rifle and tried to close the bolt to chamber a .458 round. But after about an inch it jammed, full of medium-sized quartzite sand grains from his riverbed leap. He tried again. Nothing – he couldn't budge it at all. This was now more than a tricky problem. It had become a potential life and death crisis. He screamed at the elephant 'Voetsek, Voetsek!' – a vigorous though not particularly profane Afrikaans plea to go away – and scrambled up the cliff-like face of the bank holding the now useless firearm. So there they were, all hanging on to the cliff, some balancing on improbable pebbles, others with nails dug into the sand, all very precarious. All, that is, except for the Dutch guy who had climbed to the top and seemed to be moving out of sight and into the bush. Bad move, that. The large elephant group was up there, still chasing Isaac, so once again Brett shouted for him to stay with the group.

Meanwhile the elephant cow, having reached a frenzy of anger, screaming and trumpeting, had reached a point immediately below them where she stood sniffing with her ears and trunk flapping. That she was looking for him Brett was certain. He said that he would always remember her short, sharp, perfectly straight tusks. And there he was, just above, hanging on to a few small stones for dear life. However, the two smaller elephants, as confused and panic-stricken as the rest of us, were just behind their mother – and it was to them that she turned, still trumpeting, before running back down the riverbed from where she had come, heading in the direction of the still noisy larger group of elephants.

They clambered up to the top, joined the Dutch guy and regrouped, then found Isaac and the relative safety of the vehicle. Was everyone okay? Brett asked. Nobody was really sure. Probably it had been 30 or 40 adrenaline-fuelled seconds, running, shouting and climbing. It had seemed a lifetime. Of physical signs there were many. The rifle was completely jammed and would need dismantling. The radio was scratched and the aerial broken, camera lenses had serious scratch marks and most people had small cuts and grazes. But, after some consideration it was clear they were at least physically all right.

Back at camp there was a debrief. Brett can't really recall exactly what was said, but everyone was pretty shaken. Indeed when, later, he tried to pry open the rifle bolt his hand was still shaking so much that he had to put down the tools. Later, as they drove out of the reserve, he decided that he really did not want to do the next trail. He'd had a huge fright that morning, and it made him mull over a lot of the events. Each and every encounter with Africa's dangerous game out there was completely different, and each situation warranted different reactions and actions. Walking guides must take responsibility, make split-second decisions and protect the lives of their guests. It's a big deal.

Like other really top-notch guides Brett kept turning over in his mind the events of that day. On that last morning of the trail, as they approached the vehicle, he had relaxed and was not 100 per cent focused and concentrating. Could he have spotted the elephant sooner? To this day he doesn't know. Just the day before he had pushed the boundaries with a herd of elephants in mopane (*Colophospermum mopane*) woodland. They were very relaxed, the wind was perfect and the party got very close. He had done this for photographs. That day there were no escape routes and if one of those elephants had turned around and come for them the outcome might have been very different. Was this a wake-up call from Mother Nature to respect these animals, to not push the limits, to keep the guests safe? On reflection he had done all he could not to shoot but to try and get out of the situation by other means; shouting, running, hiding and

The safest way to observe a breeding herd – from cover and height. *(Patricia Goodwin)*

climbing. Then came the time when he tried to slam that bolt closed, get the sights on the elephant and shoot to kill. But it hadn't been possible, and everyone, including the animals, had survived. Luck or fate?

After some firm encouragement from others around him Brett did walk the next trail but kept a very watchful eye on all the large grey shapes that he saw anywhere and everywhere. Events like that day do happen though thankfully they are rare. Brett has been leading trails on foot for over ten years since that day, and has never again experienced the fury of that she-devil, the elephant mother. But his group had got between her and her family. It's a thing to avoid – if you can. Although Brett has moved on in his career, he and Isaac are still very good friends today and 'Eyes' continues to lead guests through the Klaserie Reserve at Nthambo Tree Camp. Experiences like that can bring people together for life.

I've walked many trails with Brett as leader and have occasionally been extremely privileged to have him as my back-up. You'd be hard pressed to find a more knowledgeable, competent and ethical guide. So when someone of that calibre raises an issue of this kind, I and other guides should listen and keep the lesson at the forefront of our mind. Since hearing his story I've tried to ensure that all our walking guides in training recognise how difficult but crucial it is to maintain that focus right up to the moment you unload the rifle back at the vehicle or the lodge.

Most unnerving elephant stories involve females who are intensely protective of their offspring and are, as mentioned elsewhere, unpredictable in their response to what they consider a potential threat. On the other hand many bull elephants are relatively calm even when approached on foot, although they keep a watchful eye on anything approaching their space. There are exceptions. The most evident are bulls in musth and occasionally other males who simply become easily provoked with no certain explanation as to why.

'Musth' is a word probably derived from the Urdu word 'mast' meaning excitement, or literally madness. It refers to a group of behavioural and physical characteristics displayed annually or sometimes biannually by adult male elephants. Each musth episode lasts anything from a week to three or four months, and normally is seen only in bulls over 25 years old. The main features to be seen are heightened aggressiveness, increased sexual activity, a surge of secretion from the swollen temporal glands on the side of the head and dribbling, often down the legs, of strong-smelling urine with a characteristic odour. Once smelt, never forgotten.

Some bulls in musth seem to have but one thought; access to a receptive female at the earliest opportunity, and you meet them walking on what appears to be a compass bearing through the bush. It makes for a wonderfully classic African encounter. Even then they are hugely intolerant of other bulls in musth and once I saw the dominant bull in such a meeting pick up a massive tree trunk and throw it at his rival. There was much trumpeting, and a hasty retreat on the part of the smaller animal. Other bulls in this condition may be irritable in the extreme, and almost any event can trigger at least an excessive and possibly violent response. This is where serious trouble may confront walking groups and even vehicles.

This big chap is in musth. Constant dribbling of urine on the penis and down the legs is one of the classic tell-tale signs. (Maryann Williams)

Madikwe Game Reserve is in South Africa on the Botswana border some 3–4 hours from Johannesburg. At the end of 2018 an old elephant bull began to cause significant problems for lodges and their guides.

Owen Booysen had just completed a morning game drive. The guests had been delivered to the lodge for brunch, and he was looking forward to a bit of relaxation and getting some admin done when the radio burst into life. He and some other guides were required urgently to try and encourage a bull elephant to leave the lodge grounds. He was a big boy with broken tusks, and was just entering musth.

Shortly afterwards Owen plus two other guides and two maintenance guys arrived on the scene. They located the elephant in some thickets at the far end of the camp from the lodge gate, up behind the owner's house, where he had broken the fence to get in, probably enticed by better grass or juicier trees. They shouted – he moved away slowly and apparently reluctantly. They moved a bit closer, and although he continued his slow walk his posture changed. He lifted his head and spread his ears wide. A warning. After 50 metres of walking very slowly he reached the fence. And turned and charged.

Initially just a threat. Not very far, not very fast, but a charge. He repeated this a few more times. But then came the real and serious charge. One of the guides with Owen ran away, and the elephant followed him at speed. It appeared to be catching him, so Owen picked up a large stone and threw it at the animal.

This infuriated the elephant, who immediately changed direction and charged directly towards Owen. His ears were spread and he trumpeted loudly. Perhaps he was going to stop. Owen watched him carefully. At 15 metres he dropped his head and came on quickly, running right through a bush willow, splitting it in half. This time he was going all the way. Owen ran, literally for his life, zig-zagging through bushes and between trees, the elephant close behind all the while. Eventually he reached the place where the fence was broken and made a very tricky exit over it, calling to the others to see if they were OK. Also he shouted to tell them he was getting his rifle. When he did so he quickly called the wildlife department of the park. They told him not to shoot the elephant but to await their arrival, when they would assess the situation. It took their team four and a half hours to get to the lodge. The elephant was long gone. Two days later the same animal charged a vehicle on a game drive, though there was no damage or injury.

The end of the story is predictable. Reports by several guides indicated their great concern that there was a tragedy waiting to unfold. Soon after Owen's confrontation a tragedy did indeed occur. Leopard Rock is one of the Madikwe lodges, and in December 2018 the head guide and manager was Mark Lautenbach, very experienced and very highly thought of. He had returned from his honeymoon to hear that an elephant had been making himself a thorough nuisance by threatening vehicles, posturing at every opportunity, and on one occasion breaking through the electric fence that surrounded the lodge and wandering around within. Shortly afterwards the old bull made another personal appearance at the fence, and Mark went to assess the situation. The elephant promptly charged through the fence and trampled Mark. He died immediately of his injuries.

The consensus of guide opinion was that this was the same elephant that Owen had encountered. There are always inquiries after this type of appalling event, both official, and between guides locally and more widely in the general area. These are important and healthy. What happened, why did it happen and could it be prevented in the future. There was no doubt that this elephant was a serial offender in terms of disturbing the peace one way or another. At different times paint ball guns and air rifles had been fired at him and large calibre rifle warning shots aimed above his head. Could these interventions have made the elephant more irritable towards humans than usual? Was he ill or having age-related feeding problems? There is a very large number of elephants in Madikwe. Does population stress increase irritability and decrease tolerance in the animals? Lots of questions, few answers, but desperately sad.

7 CREATURES FROM THE DEEP

Sharon Haussmann is a well-known businesswoman in Hoedspruit, in the Limpopo province of South Africa. At the time of writing she is also the chairperson of the nearby Balule Private Game Reserve. This not only confirms her bush credentials but also indicates her richly deserved high standing in the community. She told me this story as an important take-home message for all those who live in or venture into the bush.

The background was straightforward. She had planned a photoshoot for a catalogue to promote her business, Khaki Fever Work Wear. This involved bringing together a team of people from Johannesburg that included four models, a photographer with his assistant and a project manager who happened to be a cousin of Sharon's. Sharon herself was there too, of course. The shoot took place in the Balule Private Nature Reserve, part of the Greater Kruger National Park and therefore a Big Five area. Given that inevitably the action would largely be on foot it seemed sensible to bring along someone with considerable bush experience who was both permitted to use, and handy with, a .458 rifle, because whilst a breeding herd of elephants or a pride of lions might make for an interesting photographic backdrop, their sudden appearance on the scene would be undesirable and potentially hazardous. The decision turned out to be literally life-saving.

The big day arrived. As it was high summer Sharon had elected to go for a 4.30 a.m. sunrise start to catch the early morning soft light. Also she wanted some shots with water as background. The key people had scouted the area for the best locations some days before and started on the shore of a dam that Sharon and her entire family knew well. It was quite shallow and had been a much used 'go-to' place for picnics and fishing expeditions. On the day it was dead calm with a surface like glass, and had good all-round visibility for early visuals of any approaching dangerous game. The whole team was very focused rather than relaxed, and everything seemed to be going well.

As the sun got higher it became clear that the photographer needed some shade to reduce direct light on the lens. The model was standing about 3 metres from the water's edge, and the project manager, Sharon's cousin, was about the same distance from the

The model poses by the waters' edge – this was the final photograph, moments before the crocodile attack. *(Sharon Haussmann)*

water, holding a jacket up as artificial shade. Suddenly a large crocodile rushed out of the water, seized her by the calf and began dragging her into the dam. She was an extremely fit and strong woman and she dropped onto all fours, digging her hands into the mud, trying desperately but unsuccessfully to stop the beast from dragging her further in. She was screaming, the model was screaming, others were shouting. It was complete mayhem.

The armed escort, who hitherto had been leaning against a wall, rifle in hand, hoping to get good views of the models, sprang into action. He quickly chambered a round but instantly recognised that blasting away at the croc was likely to cause significant collateral damage to the

In crocodiles the teeth are all visible when the mouth is closed. The 4th tooth in the lower jaw protrudes obviously over the upper lip. In alligators the lower teeth are not usually visible if the mouth is closed. *(Jeff Williams)*

woman. So he waded knee-deep into the water and managed to find a shooting angle that would both dispatch the crocodile to wherever crocs go after death and avoid hitting the woman's lower limb, now firmly inside the animal's jaws. It was all over in a couple of minutes, maybe less, unbelievably quickly.

Now they had a significantly wounded lady on their hands, blood and mud everywhere, still turmoil all around – but this is where mobile phones really come into their own, always provided there's a signal. After the call to the paramedics she was taken to meet an ambulance at the reserve gate, and she was in hospital in Phalaborwa soon afterwards. She made a full recovery thanks to good surgery and 128 stitches.

There was a lot of reflective thought about this incident. Had everyone who knew the place so well been really careless and blasé? There had never been any anxiety or moments of concern during family outings to the water's edge. Nobody could recall seeing a croc there – ever. But the incident certainly changed everyone's views, and all concerned are now considerably more cautious about accepting the safety of any stretch of water in the bush.

The Nile crocodile (*Crocodylus niloticus*) is a highly successful ambush predator. It's one of the few animals that sees humans as a potential meal, and is thought to be responsible for a large number of attacks on humans each year, though the precise number is difficult to ascertain as many non-fatal incidents go unreported. A Crocodile Specialist Group has suggested a figure of over 300 attacks per year in Africa with an estimated mortality rate of 63 per cent, but this could be a considerable underestimate. During the preparation of this book there were three well-publicised fatalities, all similar in that possibility of crocodile attack hadn't appeared on anyone's radar. In one, it seems that an 18-year-old English girl had been assured by a local lodge that the lake in which she was planning to swim was quite safe. In another instance a 38-year-old lady was sitting in very shallow water in the Okavango Delta watching her son fishing when a 15-foot crocodile attacked her. In the third case, two young golfers had wagered who could collect the most golf balls from the edge of Lake Panic in the Kruger National Park: the fatal incident affected one of them, who was standing waist-deep in the water. On the other hand guided parties on land rarely experience confrontations, though whilst a guide friend and I were walking what we felt was a safe and comfortable 20 metres from the water's edge of a lagoon in the Okavango Delta, we would have collided with a decently large croc, apparently asleep and catching some rays, had it not been for the saving grace of some not-too-tall grass. The crocodile pushed off before we got too close, showing the impressive turn of speed that always surprises me. We were particularly impressed by how high off the ground that large croc stood; as is so often the case, its back came up to around waist height. The conclusion from all this is that one should be wary of any stretch of water in crocodile territory. The lesson for all is clear. Even if you believe a body of water to be crocodile-free don't take chances. Give any inland shoreline a wide berth, and be very watchful.

✳ ✳ ✳

Now you see me, now you don't. The crocodile in the grass. *(Patricia Goodwin)*

In any inland water, even deepish mud wallows, there may be dangers much larger than crocodiles. It is commonly held that the hippopotamus kills more people in southern Africa than any other animal. There is no reliable evidence to support this contention, although this might be a function of poor collection of such incidents in the most rural areas. Forgetting the statistics, hippos certainly represent a distinct threat to certain groups of people. For local people living in villages near rivers or dams, the water is often a focal point for water collection or washing. This brings with it an increased risk of confrontation with hippos, particularly close to sunset, when the animals leave the water and to forage, and at sunrise, when they return to their safe, watery haven. This is why guided parties on foot avoid hippo trails like the plague at the extremes of the day; the simple tactic of keeping away from hippo paths or tracts of water in the early morning or late afternoon is a much better way of avoiding hippo encounters.

However sound advice this might be, all experienced guides have come across hippos lying up in mud wallows many kilometres from water; they will have been foraging overnight a long distance from home with insufficient darkness to make it back the same night. It isn't unknown for hippos to walk anything up to 5 kilometres, sometimes even further, in a night, so continual situational awareness is mandatory. With a guide colleague and students I have personally almost walked into a hippo who was resting quietly in some bushes 20 metres from the water's edge. He exploded from cover – and fortunately headed for the water and safety. We all needed to sit down for a moment after that.

* * *

Hippos can even be found strolling around in the day. This photograph
was taken at 11 a.m., at a considerable distance from water. *(Jeff Williams)*

Notwithstanding all these well-recognised issues and the care that all experienced guides
take, any one of us can get into an entirely unpredictable situation that unfolds very
quickly. Greg Esterhuysen had the great misfortune to be involved in such an incident.

It was a routine sort of bush walk along a route that Greg and many guides before
him had used over and over again without incident. I'd crossed the dam myself several
times on similar walks. The guests were slightly older than usual, all over 60 years and
some over 70. This is acceptable as long as their fitness for the planned walk has been
assessed. The group was from Europe, with a female tour guide in her mid-70s who had
lived in South Africa for many years. Some of the party spoke little or no English, and
this may have had a bearing on the outcome.

There are two obvious ways to get to the best part of the excellent walking area used
for this outing. One involves going through a depression of quite thick bush in places,
well known locally as the haunt of a pride of lions and better avoided. The second, and
much easier option, is to walk across a dam wall some 2 metres wide, steep on both
sides, with the water on the left and the aforementioned depression on the right. If the
water level is high, there is mild anxiety that someone might slip and fall in, particularly
at the 'difficult step' halfway across. Almost invariably there are hippos, and sometimes
a croc, in the dam.

And so we come to the events of the day. Greg's plan was to cross the dam wall,
as we all usually did. There was a good pre-trail briefing at the outset and appropriate
trails procedures in place with the lead guide at the front and the back-up guide
at the rear, as was the rule of that park at the time. Both guides were armed and
experienced.

The walk took place at a time of severe drought, so the water was a considerable distance away and the party crossed the difficult step without difficulty. Indeed, they were almost off the wall when suddenly Joseph, the back-up guide and walking at the rear of the party, saw a large adult hippo down to his right and way below, maybe 5 metres or more, and at least 10 metres distant. Only the front of its face and nose were visible, with the remainder of its body obscured by an embankment. Greg, using hand signals, asked Joseph to backtrack a few feet to get a better angle to understand the state and temperament of the animal. Was it even alive? The response was a low, patting hand gesture, indicating that there was a calf present.

It was at this point that things changed for the worse. Dangerous game mums with babies can lead to dangerously big trouble. However, hereabouts the dam wall on that side is high, 4–5 metres or so, and steep. This would represent a major challenge to any hippo with malign intent, though females with babies are never to be underestimated. Indeed, the hippo immediately charged the bank at almost its highest point and, unsurprisingly given the steepness, slid back down almost like a cartoon animal. Greg's response was immediate – hurry the guests off the dam wall with the back-up guide leading them to safety on the far side whilst he, Greg, would watch the hippo for any sign of threat. At that point the situation seemed well in hand, but nevertheless he had made the rifle ready for use by chambering a round.

Next time around her tactics were different and, a little further away from him, she tried to clamber up over a hippo transit path between the water side of the dam and the bush-filled depression. As soon as her head appeared at ground level from behind a bush Greg glanced backwards to check on the safety of his party. One thing you never

The Ruighoek dam wall. *(Jeff Williams)*

realise is how long a hippo's body is! Just by turning its body 90 degrees towards you, makes the animal instantly 3 metres closer! In a flash the hippo was on him, knocking him one way and the rifle the other. Behind him, chaos.

The guests, in their sunset years, didn't turn words into action fast enough. The party split into two groups, one each side of an acacia bush, with the tour leader left uncertain as to which group to follow. This hesitation left her alone, a few metres from anyone else. It was directly towards her that the hippo charged.

Being struck by an animal weighing at least 1,500 kilograms is a big, serious whack. Down went the leader onto her face, covered by the hippo. Because of the disposition of the guides, the guests, the tour guide and the acacia bush, shooting the rhino was an extremely complicated problem, though one that had to be solved. Both Greg and Joseph had to move quickly and decisively, all the while considering where the shots might go if they missed. There was no possibility of a traditional brain or chest shot. So the guides did the next best thing and fired five rounds into the animal's rump. It had the desired effect and the hippo fled the scene.

Unfortunately, the tour guide came out of this very badly with multiple injuries, though blessedly she survived. The hippo had left highly significant calling cards by standing on her thigh and chest as well as briefly sliding a foot over her head. Together these resulted in some serious medical challenges. The hippo was sufficiently badly wounded to require a careful review by the National Park staff and this resulted later on the same day in a decision to euthanise the animal. No-one ever found out the fate of the baby hippo, but it was highly unlikely to survive alone. It was a sad business all round.

Like nearly all other animals, female hippos with babies are generally much more of a threat than when they are alone. They will fiercely defend them even when the threat is theoretical, presumably on the basis that attack is the best form of defence.

After a critical incident there may be highly complex post-incident issues which can involve considerable anxiety for the guide involved. Soul-searching is common. Should I have avoided that particular area of bush on the walk? Could I have handled the situation that developed differently? Did I miss a crucial clue that danger lay ahead? And so on ad infinitum. After this period of self-flagellation it may become apparent that actually it was simply bad luck and, as mentioned earlier in the book, a 'wrong time, wrong place' situation. This self-critical review process is common amongst guides, but not all are fortunate enough to have an experienced friend or mentor with whom they can review informally and discuss any given incident. In the absence of such support guides can feel very lonely – particularly when they recognise that a given incident may trigger a local enquiry, media exposure and, in some more dramatic cases, a very public legal examination with the potential for significant criticism or, in worst-case scenarios, civil or even criminal proceedings against them. It can be a tough time.

8 BY MOONLIGHT

Selinda Spillway in 2007. *(Maryann Williams)*

Sometimes, even experienced guides sit bolt upright in admiration of the actions of a colleague who has managed a critical situation with confidence and courage if not exactly aplomb. Such was the extraordinary tale related by Kane[6] Motswana, a guide in Botswana who is rightly and intensely proud of his bushman heritage. At the time he was based at Duma Tau lodge in the Linyanti area of Botswana, and was the head guide for the Linyanti Concession.

---

6 Kane is pronounced 'Kah-nay' or for French scholars Kané.

The Selinda Spillway is a shallow channel that connects the northern Okavango Delta to the Linyanti and Chobe river systems. Until 2006 it was almost always free of water apart from occasional pools but since then, especially during years of high water, the spillway has flowed (usually May–October). It is bidirectional; depending on the relative water levels at either end, it may flow towards or from the delta. For the rest of the year it is usually dry. It is an area which contains riverine woodland and some mopane forest and so is rich in animal and bird life.

Kane Motswana. *(Kane Motswana)*

The story took place in June and it had been raining heavily. The water levels everywhere, including the spillway, had been rising rapidly. Kane had been asked by the explorations division of Wilderness Safaris (for whom he sometimes led trips into the bush) to assess the condition of the roads between Duma Tau and another camp, Keitumetse. The road was used frequently by the company to transport guests and, crucially, crossed the spillway. If all went well the drive would take about five hours. He was accompanied by Dolly, a waitress at Dumatau, who was keen to visit her boyfriend at Keitumetse. Although she lived in the bush Dolly had no experience of walking in dangerous game country, but as any walking in the bush would be a highly unlikely proposition on this journey Kane had no concern about taking her along.

That earthy and warm fragrance of rain on dry ground was in the air as they left the lodge. It was 3 p.m. and the road, a typical unsurfaced bush track, was easy to follow and well-known to Kane, who had done this journey many times before. The first three hours of the journey passed uneventfully but pleasantly with a multitude of game sightings to break what might otherwise have been monotonous driving. Groups of impala raced off the road as they surprised them, a zebra stallion watched them carefully as his harem jogged away into cover, a small group of female kudu stood quietly in some bushes and assumed they couldn't be seen; there were buffalo and roan antelope, as well as, importantly, large numbers of elephants. Elephants would figure significantly as the journey continued. Classic sightings in classic surroundings.

It soon became apparent that the crossings of the spillway and its sandy bottom, which the route required several times, had to be taken very cautiously given the amount of rain that had fallen. But at 6 p.m., on one of these crossings, the Land Rover lurched into unexpected and critically deep water and the engine died.

This was a big problem. They had covered over half the distance but Keitumetse was still some 28 kilometres distant. By now sunset was just 45 minutes or so away, and

ON FOOT IN THE AFRICAN BUSH Adventures of Safari Guides

then they would be deep in the bush, far from help, in the dark and either sitting in the vehicle awaiting rescue or on foot. Staying in the vehicle might mean being there for a considerable time before the alarm was raised as there was no radio communication in this area. And the water was clearly still rising. So Kane decided that they should walk out. Understandably, Dolly was very hesitant about leaving what she regarded as the security of the vehicle, especially as darkness was descending upon them; indeed initially she refused to move. This impasse was only overcome when Kane made it clear that the only sensible thing was to walk, that he was going anyway and that if she wanted to stay alone he would come back and get her sometime the following day, probably late afternoon. That did the trick and out she got. He explained to me later that it was infinitely preferable to press on towards Keitumetse because it was a bit closer and because there was a water supply all the way. Back towards Duma Tau there was none until you got quite close to the camp.

So off they set, following the road. As Kane said later, this was not the cleverest thing to do because lions typically use roads when travelling. But the alternative was even less attractive – walk through the bush and risk adding navigational problems to their already perilous situation. Getting lost was not in the plan.

The sun rapidly sank below the horizon and suddenly the light was gone. Almost immediately they bumped into a breeding herd of elephants feeding amongst the bushes along the edge of the spillway. 'Almost' bumped into them would be closer to the truth because Kane heard them in time, though it was impossible to sense exactly where they were and how many there might be. Elephants are spooked quite easily even in daylight. The combination of darkness and a breeding herd is a toxic mixture and one to be avoided. So they would have to go around them, cautiously and as quietly as possible. The only safe way to accomplish this involved crossing a part of the spillway and, it being winter, this unwelcome dip into water was not only cold at the time but would render them more vulnerable to heat loss from evaporation every time they stopped. When I asked Kane about the risk of crocodiles he told me that he was confident that in the very new and rising water large crocs were highly unlikely. That statement clearly defines the knowledge and confidence of the experienced guy in the bush.

The good news was that after the very wet diversion they managed to get back onto the road, so important both for ease and speed of walking. Lions roared in the distance. An ill omen? A speedy kit check was not encouraging. Between them they had a re-chargeable Maglite, a knife, one fleece and that was it. Crucially, no food. Also, the torch was low on battery power so had to be used sparingly. Not exactly ideal equipment for a nocturnal adventure of this kind. It wasn't long before the Maglite died, the blackness then only relieved by an occasional flash of moonlight.

Suddenly, something big, clearly an animal, loomed out of the darkness. It was, he thought, a lioness. Trouble. Big, muscular, aggressive trouble. The tension was huge. He grabbed Dolly firmly and shouted that she must stand still, not run, indeed not move at all from where she stood. She was terrified. The animal came closer and then charged, now identifiable as a distinct threat, perhaps not quite as serious as a lioness but still exceedingly dangerous. It was a very large female spotted hyaena, bent on attack but fortunately alone. A hyaena clan of any size would almost certainly prove fatal.

Female 'spotties' are much larger than males and average 70 kilograms with extremely effective teeth and a bite force second only to a saltwater crocodile. A formidable foe.

She made runs at him, snapping at his legs and trying to get behind him. Kane kicked at her and used the Maglite as a baton, repeatedly swinging it though failing to connect. She continued to try and bite him though never actually drew blood. At last and in desperation he followed the primal animal instinct that attack might be the best form of defence. So he unsheathed his knife and, shouting and screaming, charged the hyaena, swinging the weapon to try and wound or even kill the beast. Now this was not all what the hyaena had anticipated. She leapt back away from every knife thrust and eventually ran off unscathed into the bush with Kane in hot pursuit. When it disappeared from view Kane returned to the road where Dolly stood, shaking with fear. It was at this point, he remembers, that Dolly said that he'd saved her life.

They walked on. But by then it was 1 a.m. and all they could manage was another 30 minutes before it became apparent that Dolly was so tired that she was stumbling and falling over. They would have to stop. The safest place, Kane decided, would be up a tree even though it was feasible that a lion might try and reach them there. He quickly located one that seemed suitable and climbable and helped Dolly up to a fork. She could rest her legs there but had to hold on tightly. Around 2 a.m. a group of elephants arrived and browsed very close to them but paid them no attention. Kane explained to Dolly that

A female adult spotted hyaena. Here, with attending White-backed vultures, she is scavenging on a carcase of an elephant though spotted hyaenas are highly efficient predators in their own right. *(Jeff Williams)*

predators were wary of elephants and so would avoid them. This would make their tree that much safer. But by 3 a.m. the temperature had fallen so much that, sitting motionless as they were, the cold had become intolerable. They would have to climb down and find a warmer resting place. So, the elephants having wandered off, they got down to the ground and Kane began to plan the next bit of walking to try to locate a secure but warmer spot. The biggest danger, he thought, would come from lions and hyaenas with their keen sense of smell – indeed the last of those had already given them a big fright. So he planned a straightforward but effective evasion strategy originally taught to him by his father. Animals tracking by scent simply follow their nose just above the ground and, unlike human trackers, do not anticipate or look for tricks. So the couple walked for about a kilometre and then backtracked for 100 metres. Now came the trick. They turned off the road at right angles and walked for another 100 metres in that direction before finally turning through another 90 degrees to remain parallel to their original direction of march. Here he found a Kalahari star apple bush which offered good cover at ground level, and dug two person-sized holes in the ground. Dolly and the fleece took one, he took the other and they curled up and tried to rest. It was highly unlikely that anything following their scent along the road would find them here. It was a pity, he thought, that the fruit of Star Apples were so unpalatable to humans.

They did manage to get some sleep though it was inevitably fitful. No animals disturbed them. Just after first light Kane foraged for fruits and found small sourplums, rough-leaved raisin berries and the fruit of a jasmine creeper. Added to these he provided water lily stems and fruits and different types of ground tubers. The skills that he had learnt as a child were bushcraft at its best and together provided such a feast that they were absolutely full and could eat no more. Fortunately, there had never been a problem with water!

By 9 a.m., without further incident, they had reached Keitumetse tented camp. With minimal equipment and no rifle they had covered almost 30 kilometres on foot, much of it in the dark and all in country hostile to humans. By any standards this represents a bush walk of epic proportion.

When they returned to retrieve the vehicle the water level had risen such that it was at the level of the back seat.

From this, the sublimely professional behaviour of a bush guide at the top of his game, to the ridiculously irresponsible behaviour of a group of walking guides in training who should have known better, seems a big leap. But they did have something in common. Moonlight.

It all happened because of the frogs. The incident took place some years ago in a dangerous game area in South Africa. Large numbers of frogs had taken up residence in the small swimming pool which sat neatly between the living accommodation and kitchen dining area of the lodge. It being the mating season, every evening soon after dark a veritable cacophony of froggy mating calls, presumably reflecting a heightening of sexual frenzy, reached a crescendo that almost drowned out attempts at conversation.

On the third noisy evening, there being no guests in the lodge at the time a certain amount of alcohol had been consumed by a group of none-too-young guides. After thoroughly exploring solutions to all the international political problems of the moment, their thoughts turned to the problem of the frogs and their noise. Something, it was agreed, must be done.

The plan, like all good plans, was simple and practical. Relocate the frogs. It is true to say that the details were not very well worked out but the enthusiastic participants were not of a mind to let detail get in their way. So, fully equipped with buckets and a deal of confidence, the first and key phase of the operation got under way. The frogs, every one of them, were to be lifted from the pool into buckets prior to phase two, their onward transfer to a place of amphibian safety. Phase one quickly ran into difficulties. Lying on your belly poolside was effective for grabbing stationary or passing frogs and popping them into a bucket. The other tactic of trawling with a bucket also worked. But the group had not considered the possibility of escapee frogs who either leapt out of the buckets or swam powerfully towards the middle of the pool. Undeterred by this devious behaviour a swimming party was quickly formed and, once in the water, these still clothed frog hunters speedily mopped up the frogs in mid-pool whilst the poolside party raced in all directions in pursuit of the 'leapers'. Soon the pool was silent, and phase two, the trickier part, was in progress.

The agreed place of safety (for the frogs anyway) was a small waterhole some 400 metres from the unfenced lodge. Even with buckets it was just a short walk. It was about halfway that someone mentioned that it was dark, they were unarmed and lions had been roaring earlier not so far away. After that the pace picked up considerably and the frogs were deposited somewhat unceremoniously at the water's edge.

Then a hyaena whooped. Close by. It was only a contact call, but the problem with contact calls is that they do what they say and attract other hyaenas. A quick flash of a torch carried by one of the team revealed two bright eye-shines standing close to the waterhole. The adventurers ran, very quickly, back to the lodge and the bar. It had been, they agreed, both a resounding success and a lot of fun. After a couple of beers they also agreed that there had been at least a dozen hyaenas.

Another day dawned. Breakfast brought bleary eyes. Lunch brought a sober view that the whole episode had been totally reprehensible and contrary to the spirit of a professional guide's code of conduct. Dinner that evening brought the awful noise of mating frogs.

9 SNAKES

Most visitors to Africa have well-defined views about snakes. Many have never seen a snake in the wild, almost none have handled one, but most are certain that almost all the snakes in the country are venomous – though poisonous is often the word they use. Few visitors are indifferent; it seems that you are either fascinated by them or hate them. On the other hand, guides are usually highly enthusiastic and knowledgeable about snakes and in most circumstances keen to move them rather than allow them to come to harm. This can lead to situations that are rather more than 'awkward'.

Brent Reed is a founding director of Letaka Safaris and the Okavango Guiding School, both based in Maun, Botswana. Although he has an extraordinarily wide knowledge of all things in the bush, at the time of this saga he had a particular focus on snakes.

It was a hot February day in 2004 – St Valentine's Day to be precise – and the day before his first wedding anniversary. It was for that reason that he was visiting his wife Ashleigh at Leroo-la-Tau camp on the banks of the Boteti River which forms the western boundary of the Makgadikgadi Pans National Park. Ashleigh was managing the lodge at the time and although Brent had hoped and intended to be playing cricket in Zimbabwe that day for his local team, the Maun Hogs, she had suggested that he might live a longer and more fruitful life if he was actually with her in body and not just spirit to celebrate the big day.

Just before lunchtime he was helping the lodge staff to set the table for the guests staying there when he noticed a small gathering of Burchell's starlings mobbing a bush down by the riverbank. Clearly something was seriously provoking them. Under these circumstances the most likely suspects are an owl or a snake. Brent was fairly certain that, judging by their extremely agitated behaviour, it was probably a snake. Let's get real here. Setting a luncheon table is never going to press the excitement button of a field guide – especially, as was the case in this instance, a guide who has a particular interest in snakes. An investigation of the circumstances of the birds in the bush might be a lot more fun than the prescribed domestic duties.

The winning smile of the black mamba. *(Brent Reed)*

So after pilfering a walking stick from the lodge's curio shop Brent set off to investigate. When he got close to the smallish bush he could see the head of a rather large black mamba protruding from the top. As the bush was very close to the area where they were planning to do an evening barbecue, locally known as a braai, he persuaded himself that on health and safety reasons alone it made perfect sense to relocate the serpent. This would ensure the welfare of the guests and in any case, as he said later, he really couldn't help himself.

He could see the tail end of the mamba in the grass below the bush so dashed in, grabbed the tail and immediately began retreating to pull the mamba out. For a moment he thought there must be two snakes because as he pulled the tail the body followed but the head at the top of the bush, whilst appearing agitated, didn't move at all. It was only after he'd moved backwards for quite a distance that the head suddenly disappeared from sight. This was the moment that Brent realised that he might have misjudged the situation rather badly. He was now in sole possession of an increasingly angry 3.5-metre black mamba that he was swinging by its tail. The available tools for the task ahead were his two 70-centimetre arms and a 1-metre walking stick. Clearly the maths was not in his favour.

Brent explains the usual tactics. 'What we normally do when capturing a venomous snake is to swing the snake around by the tail to keep the hot end away from us and then use a stick to pin the head down on the ground so that we can grab it just behind the head after which the snake is under control.

Also critical in the physics of this is that the snake must be held at the thinnest part of its body where there is no muscle that can be tensed to provide a fulcrum for the muscular fore-portion of the body'.

In the heat of the moment he forgot about the last bit. Faced with a very large snake that was getting more and more upset at being swung around the garden he decided the only way to get to the head was to hold the snake higher up the body. So he pulled the snake through his left hand until he thought he was close enough to the head but just as he was about to try and pin the head the snake realised that a fulcrum had materialised and with all its pent-up fury struck at his face. Brent dodged aside but as the mamba's mouth passed it made contact with the soft tissue on the inside of his left elbow. One fang penetrated deeply whilst the other described an arc on the skin as the inertia of the strike carried the head onwards beyond him. It was blindingly obvious that things weren't going to plan so he tossed the snake down into the braai pit, an area with only a sandy floor and high sides where they made the barbecue fires at night. When he looked down at his arm he couldn't see any blood. Although he had felt the impact of the snake's head on his arm this might have meant that he'd had a really lucky escape. Then he noticed that the snake was really struggling to move properly on the sandy substrate and saw another, better, chance of dealing with it. So he jumped down into the pit and pinned the snake's head down before it could escape. But just as he bent down to grab it he felt a sudden cold, tingling sensation rush through his body right to the top of his head. By then he had managed to get hold of the snake by the head and body but when he stood up and looked down at his left arm he saw the dark button of blood where the fang had penetrated and the angry red scratch where the second fang had also drawn blood.

When he looked up he saw Ash standing on the deck up at the lodge with her hands on her hips. She did not look very happy. By now pins and needles were coming in regular waves. By this time Brent was beginning to feel very unwell. The realisation dawned that he was in a world of trouble. He walked to the banks of the river and tossed the mamba into the bushes below before walking back up the stairs towards the lodge. Ash shouted to ask if he had been bitten. He told her that he thought so and carried on walking up towards the lodge, not wanting to run and get the blood circulation going too quickly. When he got there they went to the office where the first aid kit was kept and together put a compression bandage on his arm. Also Ash put his arm in a sling to immobilise it against his chest. Brent wrote his medical aid number on his leg and described to Ash the progression of symptoms he was likely to experience – excessive salivation, difficulty breathing, difficulty talking and swallowing, flaccid paralysis of neck and limbs followed by unconsciousness and, if he was not properly and quickly treated, harp lessons.

Faced with this most serious of problems, Ash was a star. First she made radio contact with the medical rescue team in Maun who said they would meet them on the road between the lodge and town, a 170-kilometre drive. Then she put Brent into one of the game drive vehicles and set off at best speed. With a mamba bite, time is never on your side and by the time they hit the tarred road he was already having difficulty talking and was scaring the daylights out of his wife with shallow breathing.

So there they were, racing to Maun to meet the medical team, Brent to all appearances, unconscious. He was slumped on the seat but although his eyes were closed and he didn't seem able to talk or respond, he could still hear everything. Indeed, when they met the medical team on the road he could hear and was much reassured by their quiet professionalism as they loaded him onto a stretcher and began setting up a drip. He could hear Ash passing on the instructions he had given her: he was not to be given anti-venom until after he had been given steroids to reduce the chance of anaphylactic shock. He was very speedily loaded and strapped down in the ambulance and off they went, racing towards Maun and hospital.

This is the point in the story where a reader should be able to breathe a deep sigh of relief because Brent is now, surely, safe. Unfortunately the adventure was only just beginning. In Maun there was no anti-venom available in the hospital so there was a wide local enquiry of several sources including a vet and private horse owners. Eventually enough was gathered and they administered it. Immediately Brent went into anaphylactic shock, a well-recognised allergic side-effect of antivenom. The doctor stated baldly that his blood pressure was falling, falling, and that they were losing him. Large quantities of adrenaline managed to stabilise the situation. Some of his friends had heard about the incident and came rushing in to see him – remember this is Maun Hospital where there are no fixed visiting hours or restricted areas. During a short period of lucidity he made a joke about becoming a retired herpetologist before lapsing back into unconsciousness. Meanwhile an ambulance jet had been scrambled from Gaborone to take him to Johannesburg so he was taken to Maun airport on the stretcher in an ambulance. Ah, you say. Now, at last, things are looking up. Again you would be wrong.

Immigration officers worldwide can be 'sticky'. Few people make jokes with them and strict courtesy is usually the best option. But, faced with a situation where the officer concerned would not allow any further progress because Brent didn't have his passport with him, tempers began to fray. Understandably, no one in the medical support team knew precisely where at home his passport could be located. Brent couldn't tell them even though he knew. He could hear them all shouting at the immigration officer that he was going to die if he wasn't allowed through. Eventually someone went to ransack his house in the manner of burglars and managed to find the thing, by which time Brent was under the wing of the aircraft on his stretcher with the immigration official, rubber stamp in hand, close by. The passport arrived, the officer stamped it, Brent was loaded onto the plane and at last things began to move more quickly.

He was immensely relieved to learn that Ash would be allowed to accompany him for the flight. About 30 minutes en route he briefly regained consciousness and looked out to see the sun setting over the Kalahari. It was very beautiful. He turned to his wife and told her never to say that he didn't ever take her to nice places. She cried.

In Johannesburg Brent was transported by ambulance to a clinic where he was put into the 'Botswana bed', a bed apparently reserved for people with bad judgement. Even then it wasn't all plain sailing. At one stage he had a cardiac arrest and had to be jump-started (cardioversion) but after the first 24 hours it became much more straightforward even though he still required a five-day stay in ICU.

After discharge from hospital Ash made Brent retire from mamba catching with the promise that if the mamba didn't kill him, she would. It was, of course, just a coincidence that at around this time his focus of interest changed from snakes to birds.

* * *

Although it's frequently stated that a large proportion of adverse incidents involving snakes are related to handling them, the evidence is to the contrary and most are a result of the untrained and foolhardy deciding to pick up a snake or from chance encounters. Especially, this is related to walking in the dark or in the day and being bitten on the ankle after treading on or getting very close to the snake. However, Brent's story does illustrate very well that even experienced snake handlers can easily slip into reptilian hot water. It's a really, really bad plan to pick up venomous snakes unless you have considerable expertise in so doing.

Fortunately my own experiences of very serious confrontations are almost zero and my only close encounter of significance was self-inflicted. The Tuli Block is a tiny nipple of land, the easternmost tip of Botswana, sticking out between Zimbabwe to the north and South Africa to the south. It's an unusual, stony landscape of tall, rocky kopjes set in red sand, the Hardveld, with huge trees lining the boulder-strewn banks of the Limpopo. Also, it's a great place to see leopards. That's what we were doing there; honing tracking skills and trying to find one or more of these beautiful and often elusive animals.

It had been a hot day, but the desert throws up unexpectedly cold nights. We slept around the fire, radially like spokes of a wheel, each doing a two-hour guard shift to ward off unwanted intruders, notably spotted hyaenas, and to keep the fire going. Immediately available hot coffee is important at times like that. After some desultory reading by head torch during which time I seemed to be the only person awake save the sentry, sleep crept stealthily upon me, and my sleeping bag beckoned. Crucial to this story is the point that I usually slept naked in the bag, thus better preserving the wholesomeness of underwear and socks for the following day; we were travelling light. The African night sky with the Milky Way is an awesome, almost hypnotic, sight and for a few moments I lay gazing heavenward, drifting peacefully in body and mind.

Suddenly I became aware of an odd sensation. Above my right ankle something was slowly but inexorably making its way towards my knee and beyond. Gently, ever so gently, I unzipped the sleeping bag, switched on the head torch and inclined my head as if in prayer. Which indeed it may have been, for the narrow beam of light illuminated what was quite clearly a small snake making its way, in what seemed to be a very purposeful manner indeed, towards that warm and slightly moist area that no snake should ever visit. What to do? The conventional wisdom is to stay extremely still – dead still – on the basis that snakes only strike at potentially threatening movement or at clearly defined prey detected by smell. This is sound enough theoretically, but how many souls can comply with this strategy in practice especially when the family jewels are close to potentially permanent damage? What about a careful analysis of identity? I didn't immediately recognise the snake as venomous, but now didn't seem to be the time for intellectual considerations. I grabbed the serpent as close to its head as possible and jerked it upwards, flinging it backwards over my shoulder into the darkness. At least I think that was the direction it went, and next morning none of my companions whinged about a snake suddenly descending upon them from out of the heavens. Of course, this isn't a recommended way to handle snakes. In fact it was pathetic, but desperate times called for desperate measures. Which species was it? In truth I'm unsure given the poor illumination and my panic, though I distinctly remember how attractively coloured it was. I always check my shoes for scorpions and my shirt for spiders. I forgot to check my sleeping bag, and got away with it.

Even in much more scary circumstances some people react more appropriately than I had that evening. James Carne, a highly competent and experienced guide friend of mine (we trained together), has described what happened when he was out in the bush for a walk with his family, accompanied by very respected guide, Alan McSmith.

In the 1990s James had moved permanently from England to Hoedspruit in the Lowveld area of the north east of South Africa, passed his preliminary guiding examinations and was cutting his teeth as a 'jeep jockey' at a nearby game lodge in a Big Five reserve. His two sons Sam and Johnny, both wakeboarding champions, were working and training at the Umtamvona River Lodge near Port Edward in KwaZulu Natal. Having watched them there in a competition, James drove the two boys and their girlfriends Siobhan and Kelly back to Hoedspruit. The plan was to have a two-week break in the bush. For all four this was to be their first experience of being close to animals in the wild. For this initiation James had booked two days walking and two nights in a simple but comfortable tented camp belonging to Alan McSmith. First, though, there was the more mundane but necessary foray into Hoedspruit town for Siobhan, a South African girl, to buy somewhat more appropriate footgear for the bush than the Barbie-style shoes she had packed.

The camp James had chosen was in the Timbavati conservancy, part of the Greater Kruger National Park. Later that day they met up with Alan at the Timbavati gate and were treated to a splendid introductory game drive in his vintage game viewer on the way to his rustic but very comfortable tented camp. A great dinner followed, cooked by his assistant Patrick around the fire under the stars, with an early bed for the early start the following day.

The adventure started the following morning. After walking for about 30 minutes the family arrived just below the wall of a dam. There, Alan pointed out some lion tracks to them and, in bush sign language, indicated that they needed to keep very quiet. He described the tracks in a whisper, commenting that they seemed very fresh, and led the party up the quite steep wall of the dam with James bringing up the rear. Alan sat down and motioned for the rest of the party to do the same. As James clambered up he managed to trip over and generally make a lot of unnecessary noise. This which had two outcomes: firstly, the two male lions, who'd been asleep about 200 metres across the water, got up, walked away and disappeared into the bush. Secondly, the eight young cubs lying asleep against four adult lionesses woke up and started moving around. James, red-faced from his faux pas, sat down with more care next to Kelly and Siobhan to enjoy the wonderful sighting.

This awesome and peaceful sighting was short-lived. As the cubs clambered over and around the adults one of the lionesses spied the watching group across the water and the relaxed mood changed very quickly. The four females got to their feet, led their cubs to the nearest bush to conceal them and then headed around the water towards the group.

'Don't do anything: just sit nice and still,' Alan commanded, and with that both girls started sobbing. James cursed himself inwardly, wondering why on earth he'd planned the bush walk in the first place. By now, all of them (except the guide of course) had feelings ranging from mild anxiety to being seriously frightened.

The four lionesses continued to stride purposefully in their direction, growling loudly and with tails swishing menacingly. But, 20 metres in front of the group they stopped, stared, about-turned, walked back to collect their cubs and headed away. They'd made their point very forcefully. It had been an incredible experience and everyone was on a high for the rest of the day. That continued into the evening when they downed a good few beers around the camp fire, retelling the story several times with mutual back-slapping to confirm that they were all fully blooded bush gurus. They'd been put to the test, survived to tell the tale and bossed the bush – or so they thought.

Next morning brought another early and bleary-eyed start, but after coffee and rusks the now bush-hardened veterans hit the trail again. Again James was bringing up the rear. Soon the line had got a bit stretched out so he could only see Sam and Siobhan in front of him as they came out of thick bush into a clearing. Suddenly James heard Kelly scream at Alan who, of course, was leading the group from the front. Then he could see Johnny, as white as a sheet, backing away from a huge gun-metal-coloured snake that had half of its body lifted up from the ground, swaying from side to side at eye level with Johnny, all six foot of him, its black mouth open wide, ready to strike at any moment.

There was no question of it being anything other than a black mamba, by far the thickest and longest one James had ever seen, and he'd seen mambas on several occasions, including specimens at the local reptile park. His blood ran truly cold. There was nothing, absolutely nothing, that he could do. He was too far away to try and jump in front of Johnny and take the strike. The reality was that he might be about to watch his own son die in front of his eyes, a life not even a quarter lived. It hit him like a freight train. Even as James related the story some nine years later, he was intensely disturbed by the rekindled memories. 'I remember every aspect of it. It won't ever leave me,' he said.

He shouted at Johnny, 'Stand still, don't move!' Alan, who had turned around very quickly, shouted exactly the same and added, '*Everyone* stand still!' James shouted again 'It's going to drop down and move away but when it does it might come through your legs. If it does DO NOT MOVE!' Later he said that he really didn't know where he got all those words from. It was all the right stuff but as if someone else had thought and spoken them. Miraculously, and as if awaiting the cue, that is exactly what the snake did, probably not a second after James had said it. Mind you, that second felt like an eternity. It dropped down, turned around and just slid away.

They all just stood there speechless until it had disappeared completely into bush. No-one said a word for several minutes until Johnny, with just a little bit of colour returning to his face, asked James in an uncharacteristically weak voice, 'Was that what I think it was?' James nodded and gave him a very tight hug. 'Cooool!' said Johnny, his voice slowly returning to it normal loudness: 'That's amazing, I knew it was a black mamba even though I've never seen one before, not even on the telly!' By now he couldn't stop talking and laughing – situation normal. By now James could see that he was fine, not traumatised, and just buzzing from his near death experience. Also he was clearly excited about having the best pub story ever to retell when he got back home.

But James wasn't fine at all. Naturally he was intensively relieved, but later described that he felt broken inside and seriously upset that he had been wholly responsible for putting one of his sons in such a life-threatening situation. He struggled to forgive himself despite the safe outcome. If the mamba had struck and envenomated his son it would have been in either his face, neck or chest. The mamba's neurotoxic venom might in those circumstances have led to early breathing paralysis, too fast-acting to have a realistic chance of getting Johnny to the nearest hospital with the necessary life support equipment. He might have died in James' arms and that was just beyond thinking about.

It was Alan who saved the day emotionally. He had a short, morale-restoring conversation with them all. He is a self-taught philosopher and a very spiritual human being. He simply pointed out that the most feared snake in Africa had threatened Johnny and nothing had happened – no one had died – and many more wise words. Some of these faded from James' memory, possibly because he was only half-listening, too busy deciding that as soon as he got back to his new South African home and his sons and their girlfriends were safely returned to wherever they were going, he, James, would book a one-way plane ticket to London never to return. To hell with how much he had been enjoying a new life in Hoedspruit. There was no way it would ever be worth risking putting one of his children in such danger again by continuing to live in the bush – his mind was made up.

Fast forward ten years. James is still in South Africa and still living in the bush. Now he and his wife are managing their own lodge, Sausage Tree, in the Balule Conservancy near Hoedspruit, and part of the Greater Kruger National Park. Somewhere along the line the bush magnet overcame his immediate thought of leaving, and Alan's philosophy helped resolved the parental trauma.

James added a postscript to the event. He hadn't in all his subsequent guiding career had any other dangerous wild animal or specifically snake-related experiences, including removing Mozambique spitting cobras from the lodge, that could even start to compare with this one. Also, many black mamba sightings later, he had never seen one that came even close to the size of what was a true monster specimen. He is fairly sure that it was over 4 metres in length, but more impressive was its girth, at least twice that of any other mamba he had ever seen. On a positive note, Johnny's story almost always trumps any other near-death story in the pub.

The black mamba is a bad snake to be bitten by. It has a very complex venom profile, the most potent being a neurotoxin that causes muscle paralysis, the critical muscles being those of the diaphragm which maintain breathing. There is also a 'dendrotoxin' which is highly toxic to the heart as well as other toxins of rather less importance. There are no very reliable statistics for deaths from snakebite in South Africa but an estimate of between 10 and 12 cases annually has been suggested. The most frequent culprits are the cape cobra and black mamba, though infrequently there are also recorded fatalities from snouted cobra, boomslang and puff adder. On the other hand the snake causing the majority of serious but non-fatal snakebites in South Africa is the Mozambique spitting cobra, particularly because of its penchant for entering buildings. The best plan for avoiding an unpleasant incident is to carry a torch at night, and if you meet a snake in daylight, don't approach nearer than 5 metres at the very closest, at which distance you are reckoned to be safe. Even the notorious and somewhat maligned black mamba doesn't deliberately chase people – it is, rather, a nervous individual who would much prefer to head for safety if it can. The stories of being chased may well result from that quest for safety being in the storyteller's direction. Interestingly, one description of the mamba that someone once passed on to me was of a 'beautiful grey snake with a winning smile' – I noted at the time that this attractive-sounding definition omitted the other well-known descriptive feature, the coffin-shaped head.

10 LEARNING THE GAME

Whatever your views about how dangerous a confrontation with a rhinoceros might be, in the case of a male white rhino weighing up to 3,000 kilograms it's a big beast to fall out with. But just considering their size or, as quoted by some authors, an implication that they are of limited intelligence has no scientific basis and might seriously underestimate the animal. It does seem that their eyesight is on the poor side, though precise assessment with a Snellen vision chart might prove awkward in practice. Indeed, some recent research suggests that it is rather better than we thought, though we don't know for certain exactly how much better.

Although they compensate for their vision with sensational abilities in hearing and much better sense of smell, I believe that this visual difficulty makes them very curious and, having established roughly where you are with these other sensory modalities, they may circle around you to try and clarify your position. This looks and can feel intimidating when you're on foot but shouldn't be regarded as an ambush waiting to happen.

As for the oft-quoted view that black rhinos are more bad-tempered and/or aggressive than their white rhino relatives you will hear differing views. I believe that much of it is situational and often related to curiosity. Black rhinos are largely browsers and live in close country where there are lots of bushes for food as well as cover rather than on the plains. This heightens the possibility of walking parties bumping into one. Under those circumstances often the animal will panic and run. Anywhere. There then is an approximately 25 per cent chance that it will run in your direction.

Given the current desperate plight of rhinos from poaching, most guides are extremely reluctant to shoot one even when it's a serious charge, and will opt whenever possible to take avoiding action. Ultimately, protecting the guests is the guide's top priority whatever tactic is used, though one highly experienced guide friend of mine has suggested that faced with this decision he might well rather take the hit himself and avoid shooting the animal.

With all these thoughts parked somewhere easily accessible in the brain, I cast myself back to that enjoyable phase of walking guide training when someone else carried the responsibility and we, the trainees, strolled almost contentedly behind. Contentedly, that was, until it was our turn, usually unarmed, to lead from the front for the first time. Even though our mentor would be immediately behind and ever-watchful this was, for sure, a tense time. I remember it oh so well. It took place in the non-public area of a South African National Park.

We saw the female black rhino with her small calf one ridge and some 500 metres distant. 'This is a rare opportunity – don't let it pass, go for it,' said my mentor encouragingly on this, my first day of leading a group on foot in the bush. I felt uneasy about accepting this challenge on a couple of levels. To start with I had just embarked on an earnest and, I felt, both academic and fascinating discourse on very low-frequency communication between elephants, a breeding herd of which we'd been watching from the safety of a reassuringly high and particularly steep kopje. Secondly, I detected a just discernible hint of alarm about this prospect from the 'guests', all fellow students whose moment in the sun would come later in the week. Inevitably though, notwithstanding the delicate balance between much-lauded success and abject humiliation, either of which might encompass this proposed adventure, I was too cowardly to decline or deflect the opportunity, and so off we set.

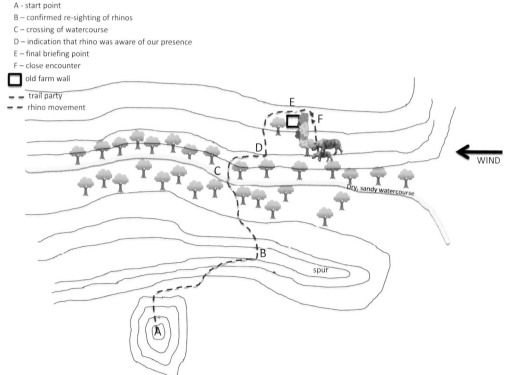

Legend
A - start point
B – confirmed re-sighting of rhinos
C – crossing of watercourse
D – indication that rhino was aware of our presence
E – final briefing point
F – close encounter
□ old farm wall
- - trail party
- - rhino movement

Jeff's rhino confrontation.

As the day warms up many animals, especially black rhino, seek shade. This is a wild olive, a fine resting place for a rhino. The author has seen one right here. *(Jeff Williams)*

The descent of the north side of the kopje down to a small, dried-up watercourse was uneventful if laborious in the extreme, and crossing it, to ascend the slope of the low ridge ahead, free of drama. Before reaching the crest, a level area of sandy soil brimming over with tracks reminded me vividly that 'here be dragons'. Elephant, lion, white rhino – they'd all been there. All that was needed now was a couple of really irritated dagha boys and my cup of anxiety would be overflowing. I imagined my onward journey in search of the black rhino punctuated with flank attacks from large beasts intent on our destruction. This might be the guiding version of Rorke's Drift, though with no prospect of a VC before breakfast.

However, once established on the ridge, to my surprise not only were the mother rhino and child still in sight but they'd settled down to sleep under a very prominent and tall wild olive some 250 metres in a direct line from our position. Now this was much better news and my spirits and confidence grew; indeed grew sufficiently to deliver a firm briefing in the 'we *will* see the rhino' assertive, military style. We were directly south of the rhinos and separated from them by a deep, dry and potentially hazard-rich eroded watercourse, better known to those in the bush as a donga. The best plan seemed to be a westward and downwind march, crossing the donga carefully in the most open area I could find, and then working back towards the target eastwards and upwind. The assessor nodded encouragingly and the 'clients' seemed relaxed. Now, Jeff, steady as she goes. 'Plan your walk, walk your plan'; Frank Bouwer, a superb guide and teacher, often used this mantra and I have tried to follow it ever since.

It was quite thick, that walk down to the riverine, but the bush was quiet, the group closed-up and the pace OK. There was a moment's alarm when a slender-tailed mongoose bolted into some vegetation, but then there, just ahead, was the watercourse with not-so-steep banks and decent visibility both ways. We crossed and re-grouped on the opposite bank. No hesitation now. Thank goodness the wild olive was still clearly visible. There aren't many things more embarrassing on an approach than suddenly being unsure of the location of the animals.

Then the moment when things changed. From out in front came a distinct noise. A rhino noise. A rhino-that's-just-pinged-me sort of noise. What to do? Well, height is power and maybe safety, so quickly but quietly uphill to the north for a short distance before resuming the eastward course. This would bring us to a clump of trees and some tallish vegetation, the site of a farm in the old days, where now just a couple of broken walls bore mute witness to its existence. All that remained was the final briefing before the last leg of the approach.

I gathered the group all about me and in a low, conspiratorial sort of whisper delivered the key messages. 'The rhinos,' I said, 'are some 50 to 60 metres away, close to that tree where we saw them before. Given a bit of luck, there'll be sufficiently good visibility to get photographs, so get those cameras armed and ready. Is everybody up for this? Great. Then keep close, keep quiet and keep in single file. Remember the default action in an emergency. Stay behind the rifle, close together and obey implicitly and immediately whatever instruction I give. Are we good to go?'

I'm not entirely sure who was the more surprised, me or the rhino, when I left the safe haven of the trees and, five paces later, walked round a bush to come face to face with her 7 metres away (I measured it later). We stared at each other for a fraction of a second and she ambled towards me in a short-sighted, curious sort of way. It was never a charge. Indeed she had a 'what on earth are you doing here?' look about her. I turned to my mentor, riding shotgun as it were immediately behind me, and (as he said subsequently in the debrief) pointed a thumb over my shoulder in a somewhat over-calm sort of way and uttered the immortal words 'She's just here.'

To this day, the events that ensued remain a bit of a blur. I recall rifles being shouldered, the armed back-up springing forward to present a consolidated front, much shouting, which included an exhortation in extremely down-to-earth barrack-room language for the guests to find some cover, and the slapping of hands on magazines and stock to persuade the animal that retreat was strongly advised. The rhino, not overly impressed with the whole business, turned and ambled off rather unhurriedly with her baby, who'd read all the textbooks and stayed firmly behind mother.

I needed to sit down for a moment after that, and we took this time as an opportunity to review the incident. The two colleagues at the rear of the line asked what it was that had caused the commotion, as they hadn't seen any animals at all. Another complained bitterly that he'd run through a sickle bush and needed first aid, and yet another, a particularly tall chap, claimed to have seen the beast over the top of the bush but he'd whistled quietly to avoid disturbing the animal. By now I'd accepted that this was an inept performance and awaited the damning verdict.

Face to face. At 7m distance, even a black rhino female has a formidable presence.
(Jeff Williams)

'Best sighting of black rhino that I've had for years,' said the boss, smiling just a little. 'Mind you, it was a bit close. We both should have considered the possibility that she'd moved, and got ourselves into a better position to see round that thicket before boldly stepping out where no man has been before.' I found smiling a tad difficult for more than a few minutes. Indeed, although it was more than 15 minutes since the incident, my legs shook every time I tried to stand up. It was a very, very close call.

Every guide will make at least one mistake at some point in their career. The important thing is to recognise what happened, how it happened and what steps should be taken to prevent it happening again. So mentally replaying the whole sorry saga over and over again shouldn't be regarded as indulgent self-flagellation but accepted as an essential tool for an otherwise confident and thoughtful guide. Also, it then makes it much easier to pass on any useful tips to fellow guides who, in my experience, never laugh at your misfortune but listen very, very carefully. Mind you, I've never had to relate this incident. Everyone in the Park seems to have heard about it. 'Aren't you the guy who walked slap bang into a black rhino?' comes immediately after the introduction and simultaneously with the handshake. At that point I usually quote Oscar Wilde: 'Experience is the name that everyone gives to their mistakes.'

✳ ✳ ✳

Occasionally, as part of the curriculum for training walking guides, we take them to places where we would not take guests. This is a lesson worth learning. The area we most commonly use for this are the thickets at Leeuwfontein (Chapter 4) for 'Here be tigers' – not literally of course.

On one occasion whilst on such a walk we happened upon the spoor of an exceedingly large lion. The tracks disappeared into the thickest of all thickets, which no guide of sound mind would even consider entering. Even crouching to peer inside made us nervous; it was that sort of place. Making a plan was straightforward. He had to emerge somewhere. So if we walked a moderately wide circle we should cross his track, unless he had remained within. We did walk the circle: we found precisely nothing. That is until we completed the 360 degrees and found that, during our circuit, he had retraced his steps and cut our trail. We followed this newer, indeed very recent, spoor which led us to a rocky outcrop where we promptly lost it again. Ah well, that's the bush, we all decided.

But my boss, the lead guide on the day, had other ideas. 'Lions like roads,' he said. 'On the way to the vehicle [parked on the road] we'll see if we can pick up the big guy again.' Off we walked at a slower, steadier pace, increasingly alert and not a little excited by now, towards our Land Cruiser. Some minutes later we reached the parking spot, and there came across the biggest statement that an animal can make to a guide. There, encircling the vehicle were the prints of a very large lion, apparently the 'big guy'. After his circuit he had peed on one of the wheels. Probably the biggest F*** YOU statement he could think of!

✳ ✳ ✳

Sometimes the lesson we learn is because of someone else's situationally wrong call though it's just as important a learning point. Jo Cooper now operates overland safaris in southern and eastern Africa and described a great example of this.

The camp-out on his Trails Guide course had been great fun and much more interesting for the students than classroom work, especially as there was always the possibility of unplanned encounters with potentially dangerous animals. But the incident he described was more or less planned – they knew exactly what they were going to see and roughly where they were going to see it.

It had started so typically. A group returning from a walk had reported a sighting of some lions lounging under a tree and had given decent enough directions, so six trainee guides, including Jo, set out on foot with their instructor to get a slice of the action. In the event they came across the lions rather abruptly, rounding some bushes and confronting them from about 20 metres. Unsurprisingly, that brought them to an abrupt halt. There was a large and rather grand male named Shaka plus two of his sons, each about two years old. That's old enough to kill prey and old enough to behave like a testosterone-fuelled teenager whose toes you've inadvertently just trodden on.

Between the lions and the group there was just flat, open ground. The wind was positively unhelpful and they caught human scent immediately, lifting their heads by way of acknowledging the presence of interlopers before lying down again, apparently uninterested.

'They seem pretty relaxed; let's stay here awhile,' suggested the instructor, the lead guide. So they did and sat down comfortably on the ground.

It only took five minutes before it all went very wrong. One of the younger lions suddenly stood up and started to walk towards them, growling all the way. This was the onset of trouble with a capital T. In South African parlance it would be termed 'hectic'. A shout of 'stand up and back off' got the guides moving, but as soon as they did so the large bulk of Shaka also arose and came steadily in their direction. The growling became louder. Much, much louder. Very soon all three lions were approaching from different directions though they stopped at about ten metres away. That was close. Then they moved closer together and the growling and threatening posture became very intimidating. Jo and his colleagues stood their ground and shouted back at them, this stand-off lasting for a few minutes. When next they tried to back off the lions came even closer, and this process was repeated time after time. The whole party was very, very anxious, Jo said, though I suspect this was an understatement.

Meanwhile, back at camp the roaring and shouting had become audible and prompted a rescue mission. But. just as in critical situations in movies, the vehicle coming to their aid got stuck in the sand of a dry riverbed. More delay, more roaring, more anxiety. Jo described how dramatically his heart was pounding, and he could feel the sheer power of the lions reverberating through his chest. At last the rescue party arrived, probably 20 minutes after they had set out. Shaking, sweating and with knees like jelly the group climbed aboard. It had been a truly terrifying experience.

After situations like that there is always a debriefing. What had gone well? Not a lot really. They had found the lions and nobody (including any of the lions) had died, but everyone agreed that they'd been too close to stay and gaze at the always awesome sight of three beautiful and apparently relaxed predators. But all potentially dangerous animals must be regarded as predictably unpredictable. Their behaviour yesterday – or even a few minutes ago – shouldn't be considered as their likely behaviour now. Another day in the bush, another bush lesson learnt.

11 SIMPLE PLEASURES

Whoever you are and wherever you live there are so many things you do that can be regarded as simple pleasures of life. These might include a relaxing swim after a long day, a picnic with family and friends, a walk with your partner or even picking the kids up from school. But set these normal events in the context of the African bush and things may take a very unplanned turn.

North Luangwa is a comparatively little visited and remote national park in Zambia of over 4,500 square kilometre, not open to the public and with no permanent lodges. A little while ago I had a most pleasant walk there with professional walking guide Rod Tether. We concluded the outing at a delightful spot at some waterfalls on the Mwaleshi river, attractively sited on the edge of an escarpment and a favourite spot of his. It was pleasantly cool under the beautiful overhanging trees but with rays of warm sun piercing the canopy and so not too cold in the water. Having a swim after a long and active hot day seems a disarmingly straightforward thing to do, but it was there that Rod told me of the unplanned encounter he had experienced in these very pools.

It was getting towards the end of the dry season of a very dry year. Skeletal outlines of deciduous trees were dotted across the landscape and parched brown leaves hung listlessly from the thorn bushes. Rod was guiding his guests to the very pools described above. It was a big day out, comprising an early start with a couple of hours of driving through the park before setting off on foot through some fairly arid mopane woodland for another few hours or so. By the time you reach the falls a refreshing dip in the pools is always very welcome. As usual he had a fairly mixed group but most people eagerly seized the opportunity to cool off by leaping into the waters that had been deemed safe. Theoretically, the water was flowing too swiftly for a crocodile-friendly environment, but even so he'd checked around quite carefully, to be on the safe side.

One of the party could not be tempted into the water. He was an elderly gentleman who had lived in Zambia for a few months in the sixties and considered himself as something of an expert on all things wildlife. He was at pains to remind Rod that in Africa you never swim in water that you can't see the bottom of.

Now Rod always liked to give his guests some space at this spot so, after some time messing around in the water with them, took himself off to a lower pool, about 10 metres by 5 metres in size, thereafter dropping off almost vertically to the next, rather larger, pool below. These days we'd call it an infinity pool. With the gentleman's advice fresh, indeed ringing, in his ears he checked the sides of the pool for slides that might indicate crocodile activity and regarded it studiously for five minutes or so. Nothing. Not a movement, not a ripple, not a bubble, nothing. By way of reassurance he reminded himself that if you were to restrict swimming in Africa to places where you could see all of the bottom, all of the time, you would end up limiting the activity to private and municipal swimming pools.

So he took the plunge, literally, and swam gently with the current the short distance to the lip of the pool where it dropped away. Just as he reached it he sensed, more than felt, a sort of stirring right beneath his body. The next moment he was hit, hit hard, on the right elbow. On the assumption that it was a croc and unsure whether he'd been hit or bit, he swam as fast as he could over the very short distance back towards the shore. He glanced over his shoulder and there, terribly close, was a large mouth literally inches from his face. He registered the pink-coloured inside of the mouth and facial hair but it was still a croc in his head. As his feet touched solid ground he raced out, turning around as he did so – but there was nothing, absolutely nothing to see.

Rod must have shouted or even screamed, for, alarmed by the commotion his scout had come running down with his rifle and together they watched the water for between 10 and 15 minutes. Then, almost imperceptibly, a pair of large nostrils emerged – no ears, no eyes, just nostrils, but enough to confirm that it was a hippo.

The hippo's nose and ears are evident to an observer on the bank. Looking over your shoulder and swimming for your life you see what you expect to see. (*Jeff Williams*)

Later, Rod took the guests on a walk upstream, and while they were away the scout and tea-bearer couldn't resist the temptation of getting the hippo out of its hole by hurling rocks into the water.[7] They reported that it was a big old bull, badly injured down its flanks from what would have been a fight with another hippo. This was presumably the vanquished male who, having lost his watery territory plus his mating rights, now sought shelter wherever he could find it in this driest of dry seasons when sufficiently deep pools for large hippos were difficult to come by. He could have killed Rod. A quick chomp from that massive gape and Rod would have been a goner. Luckily, the hippo had chosen to give just a gentle, perhaps even affectionate, nudge after Rod had swum directly over him – and the only damage was a slightly bruised arm and more than slightly bruised pride.

To his credit the old guy said nothing publicly or privately, though in his eyes Rod thought he saw just a hint of 'I told you so'.

Calvin Cottar is one of East Africa's most renowned private guides and represents the fourth generation of a family has been running safaris in Kenya for 90 years. His great-grandfather Chas arrived for a hunting safari in what was then British East Africa in 1909 after reading Teddy Roosevelt's book *African Game Trails*. He was so taken with it all that he moved his family there from his home in Oklahoma. Chas' three sons were outfitting and guiding safaris in Africa and India 20 years before the Blixen/Denys Finch Hatton era of 'Out of Africa' fame. Many of their clients were famous and included George Eastman of Kodak and the British royal family.

Calvin's parents, Glen and Patricia Cottar, continued this pioneering spirit. In between operating hunting safaris all over Africa, they opened the very first permanent tented safari camp exclusively for photographic clients in Tsavo East in Kenya in 1964 – at the time, everyone thought they were crazy! A couple of other tented camps followed and subsequently Calvin and his wife Louise opened Cottar's 1920s Mara Safari Camp in 1998, at the time of writing still operating.

It was Calvin who told me a tale of a simple outing in the bush planned as a family picnic. It turned out to be no picnic at all.

Peter Hill Beard (1938–2020), the internationally famous American photographer, artist, diarist and writer, is the other main participant of the story. He had many of his African experiences whilst on safari with Calvin's father Glen and, when hunting in Kenya was stopped in 1977, he had the extremely sound idea that photographic safaris could be shown to the world as being just as exciting as hunting itself. As this, in turn, might generate more interest in safari holidays, he decided to make a documentary showing just how exciting it could be. To this end, Peter managed to get the ABC network interested in making a couple of 60-minute programmes with himself as host so, in the early 1980s, he came out with a film crew to Cottar's camp in the Maasai Mara, Kenya.

---

7 This was unacceptable behaviour, and Rod was appropriately unhappy about it.

Glen's job was to guide the team to the general area of the selected dangerous wildlife for the day and then position the camera crew as close as possible, allowing a margin of safety, to film the animals. These included elephant, lion, rhino and buffalo, a decent selection of some of the Africa's most dangerous beasts. Even now Calvin remembers clearly a discussion between his father and Peter about how close they were getting to the animals despite his father's warnings that it was endangering the rest of the crew: 'Peter, you're brave and you can outrun everyone. That puts the rest of us at risk.' As a result, when they had wrapped up that film, Glen told Peter that he wasn't prepared to guide for the next film in the series.

Peter went on to commission an old friend of Glen's, Terry Mathews, for his next film and on the first day of filming Terry was injured by a rhino. Calvin was never privy to the particular circumstances of the accident, but his dad's comments about it were along the lines of 'I told you so'. Much to Calvin's disappointment this broke the friendship between Peter and his father. Peter, he says, was such a friendly and colourful fellow, always with crazy things happening around him.

Years passed but after his father Glen died Calvin reconnected with Peter in Nairobi and in 1998, Peter's 60th year, invited him to come on safari to the new Cottar's camp. One day into his stay it was decided to go to a beautiful waterfall on the Sand River for a picnic lunch: two cars fully loaded with family, photographers, friends, swimming gear and, of course, beer – though the latter had nothing to do with the near-catastrophe that followed.

After a time and when the outing was in full swing, Calvin spotted a breeding herd of elephants and suggested that for old times' sake that they, just he and Peter, should pop out and have some one on one time with them. They were driven a little closer and then they set out on foot. On the approach towards the elephant group there was a light wind very much in their favour, and they were able to get reasonably close using a large termite mound to peer over at the animals which were some 40 metres away. With no alarms and some photographs in the bag Calvin and Peter then moved quietly and easily parallel to the animals as they walked slowly away up a slope, keeping a healthy distance of 200 metres or so from them. At that point the elephants had shown no recognition of or at least any concern about the human presence.

Many elephants mistrust humans as they may have been persecuted when competing for resources, like an attractive vegetable crop, or when hunted for their ivory. More commonly they are anxious about the welfare of their young or even, in the case of bulls, bad-tempered because they are in musth. Whatever the reasons behind their decision, which may never be decipherable, when they decide to charge the chances of escape are poor unless you are able and prepared to shoot them. They can run faster than humans. They can go through any foliage in a straight line, reach up to you in a tree, dig you out of a warthog hole or fish you out of a river – all with the intention of hurting or killing you. The best way of handling this is to avoid a charge in the first place. Fine words, usually said after the event.

All was going well until the moment when, as it often does in the bush, the wind started to circulate and change direction, increasing the possibility that the elephants

The picnic site by the falls of the Sand River. *(Calvin Cottar)*

would get their scent, freak out and run away – or charge them. The elephants picked up the pace marginally, not obviously alarmed, but probably now aware that there were indeed humans in close proximity. Calvin was at pains to set the record straight that while he normally carried a rifle on walks in the bush on that particular day he did not have one because they were within the national reserve. Carrying a rifle there was not only illegal but could have got them targeted by an anti-poaching team that was known to be in the area. So they had no weapon but very considerable combined experience of elephant behaviour.

Suddenly, a cow at the back of the line wheeled around, spotted them immediately and screamed. If this scream seems to be directed at you it's a bad moment and a moment for action. Elephants' eyes are naturally positioned to be looking at what they are feeding on, on or near the ground. When they mean business they raise their head to sight the danger in this manner and to get what is in effect a good directional aim for a charge should they decide that's necessary. This was a major indicator of impending danger to Calvin and Peter, but they didn't panic – well not immediately.

On seeing them and presumably regarding them as a threat the female elephant quickly gained momentum and ran at pace to some raised ground 70 metres from them, where she slowed almost to a standstill. For their part they walked rapidly away, sideways, watching her very carefully and talking to her in steady, reassuring tones, telling her that they were not a danger to her, really, really. Sometimes this works, but that day she was in no mood to listen. Then she finally made up her mind, put her head down and came flat out towards them. Being too far from their vehicle to have any realistic chance of reaching it and with no rifle, they made a break towards it hoping all the while that the driver had seen the drama and was on his way to deflect the elephant. No such luck. Fear had frozen him to his seat and the only thing he was able to contribute was to keep his hand on the horn!

They ran together. Calvin could sense the ominous bulk of the angry elephant bearing down on them as if they were standing still, and realised that one or both of them was going to get clobbered. When she was within 'trunk reach' Peter abruptly veered left towards a termite mound and Calvin veered right, stumbled, and crashed to the ground head first fully expecting the elephant to skewer him with her shiny and pointy tusks. He had, literally, run faster than his legs could carry him: they hurt for a week afterwards!

When Calvin looked around he saw that the elephant had gone for Peter instead. She was in the backside up, head down, skewer position and he knew that Peter must be somewhere underneath, probably smashed to a pulp.[8]

Momentarily he considered grabbing the tail to distract her, but common sense prevailed and he turned and ran for the car. After hauling the driver out he took the wheel and raced back to the elephant and Peter. Meanwhile the rest of the elephant

8 A review of a video taken at the time confirmed that the elephant had a newborn calf that they had not seen and which probably explained the female elephant's aggressive behaviour. Peter and Calvin agreed that there should be no retribution against the elephant by the Kenya Wildlife Service as it was not her fault. It was just a typical bush life situation. These things happen. But this raises another question. You could argue that animals are never 'to blame' for these adverse incidents. We as guides or tourists are treading on their turf and must do so at our own risk.

Calvin Cottar. *(Calvin Cottar)*

family had arrived, galvanised into action by the screams of their mother or sister or daughter. Seven or eight of them, all trying to get a piece of the action, screaming and wheeling, dust swirling, truly a terrifying sight. But as the car approached they dropped their tails and trunks and headed back up the slope. The dust settled and Calvin fully expected to see Peter very flat and very dead. But, lo and behold there he was, popping up out of the settling dust like a jack-in-the-box, covered in dust and blood.

Typically, his first words to Calvin were 'S*** Curley, it looks like my screwing days are over!' (Calvin's nickname had always been Curley because he hadn't a hair on his head, let alone a curly one). The elephant had tried, and partially succeeded in skewering him. One tusk had gone through his thigh, just missing the femoral artery. But the real damage had been done by her nose as she slammed down on him, a common form of elephant attack, crushing his pelvis. This was a serious injury and needed immediate medical intervention. At that time Peter said that he was going blind, a dark fog crossing his eyes, the only time anyone had seen him truly afraid. Luckily Calvin knew that this was often associated with severe trauma, particularly with blood or fluid loss, and was usually self-limiting. He told him not to worry, that his sight would come back in a few minutes though it might last rather longer. Thankfully he was right and it soon improved.

From there it was a matter of getting Peter to hospital and a radio call was sufficient to arrange for the flying doctors to meet them at an airstrip 20 kilometres away. They 'bundu-bashed' through the bush and across two rivers to get there. By that time he needed urgent expert resuscitation having probably lost considerable blood with a falling blood pressure. Indeed Calvin described him as being in an almost 'dead on arrival' condition. At the time Peter was a very strong man with the constitution of an ox. Calvin recalls that during the entire journey to the airfield he was either bellowing from the pain or cracking jokes! Subsequently he walked with a titanium-patched pelvis that didn't seem to slow him down at all.

It was some years later, when Calvin brought the story to my attention, that he pondered the question of what he'd learned from the situation. 'Never think you know animals' was his first comment. He went on to say what has been reported a number of times in this book: 'Every animal can do the opposite of what you have seen him or her do 1,000 times before.' Then he talked about being armed with an appropriate rifle when walking in dangerous game areas. He believes you should always carry one, and since that incident walks in the bush with his father's (and grandfather's) Rigby .500

Nitro Express side lock double rifle. Many guides agree with this view on the grounds of it adding a level of security for both guide and client. But there are those who look at it differently. They suggest that carrying a rifle can give some guides a false sense of security and might make it rather more likely that they would push the boundaries in a given situation. I suspect that there is no right or wrong answer, just different opinions.

A final thought

In this and in other books you come across tales of people running away from elephants. But elephants move extremely quickly. Just how quickly has been the subject of much speculation for over 100 years. Even now, some professional guiding associations quote figures for the charging speed of an elephant that have no foundation in fact and are based on anecdotal observations made a long time ago.

But clarification is now at hand. Recent careful research done by Prof John Hutchinson of the department of basic veterinary sciences at the University of London has provided evidence of the fastest reliably recorded speed that an African elephant can attain. This is 6.8 m/sec or 24.5 kph (15 mph).

For guides and, more importantly, the slowest guest in a crisis, this has to be compared with man's best performance over a short distance. For this we turn to the sprinter Usain Bolt who touched 12.4 m/sec or 44.7 kph (27.8 mph) over the fastest 20 metres of his record-breaking 100-metre sprint in 2009. For normal, non-competitive but fit adults, the fastest speed they are likely to achieve on a track is considerably slower. Now throw in a standing start and substitute the bush for a track … You are not going to outrun an elephant.

As well as my mentor, boss and friend Bennet de Klerk, there are several guides who, whenever I am privileged to go out for a bush walk with them, inspire not just excitement but the certainty that it will be exceedingly interesting and fun even if we encounter not a single mammal, reptile, bird, arthropod or even tree. They will always have insights about the bush itself, sometimes very profound, to continually entertain the participants.

Such a man is Frank Bouwer now, hopefully only temporarily, lost to guiding by flying balloons in Australia. When eventually I managed to persuade him to recount an exciting bush incident he came up with this one which falls neatly into the Simple Pleasures category with just the same measure of adrenaline-fuelled action as the others but also with a necessary touch of humour to dilute the drama. It took place in the same area of Pilanesberg National Park as the events recounted in Chapter 4, and he describes it with typical understatement as 'just an afternoon stroll with friends'.

The shadows were already leaning eastwards as they disembarked from the vehicle, the heat of the day slowly dissipating. The plan was to take an afternoon walk through the part of the reserve known as Leeuwfontein for a very simple reason; because they could. It was a small party – three guides, Frank's wife and the brother of one of the other guides – so they only took one rifle, with absolutely no intention of using it. There is always something surreal about moving quietly through moderately dense vegetation in the presence of dangerous animals, heart pumping, skin prickling; and the one thing that Leeuwfontein has in spades is dense vegetation. The scent of dust and a smorgasbord of sound heighten the sensation.

The small group was drifting along slowly through the bush, going nowhere in particular, just walking, when a distinctive sound nearby caught their attention. The soft thud … thud … thud of elephant droppings hitting the ground came from the right front. Hand in the air, the lead guide signalled 'Stop'. The minutes ticked by as they stood stock still, listening, trying to locate the elephant. Then with the swish of a tail the animal sprang into focus. The elephant was a bull, judging by its silhouette visible through the bushes about 100 metres away, head hidden by the vegetation as he fed.

At that moment a decision was taken that would have interesting though undesirable consequences. They decided to get a closer look. It was a difficult approach with an adverse breeze blowing from behind them and their visibility somewhat obscured by head-high sweet thorn bushes. So they approached cautiously. After 50 metres they broke into a clearing and saw the bull moving steadily in their direction, ears spread and very purposefully. He knew they were there. Streaks of secretion from his swollen temporal glands were visible on his cheeks and the realisation hit home. He was indeed a bull and he was in musth. And they recognised him immediately – he was bad news. A charge might well be on the cards especially as elephant bulls in that physiological condition have their mind on one thing only and it certainly isn't being tolerant to humans invading their space.

As the bull disappeared into a clump of vegetation near the party they turned and ran to their right in a tight group across the wind for about 400 metres – slap bang into a herd of buffalo. They had been drowsing peacefully in the deep shade of a grove of large wild olive trees. As you can imagine this had a profound effect on the buffalo, who leapt up, or as near as buffalo can get to that, mooing and grunting. A stampeding buffalo herd can cause serious harm, flattening anything in their path, from vegetation to people unselectively. You don't wait to find out whether this is going to happen. Frank and his friends threw caution to the winds and bolted straight through the herd, laughing like lunatics as hysteria kicked in Fortunately the buffalo took off upwind as is their wont, so their paths diverged.

The party ran until they were well into a broad, chest-high strip of yellow thatching grass that grows on the savannah coming off the nearby mountain. Chests heaving and hearts racing, they stood and looked back the way they had come, trying to discern any following danger. There was nothing to see.

After a few minutes they decided that discretion was the better part of valour and, as it was getting late, planned to skirt the edge of the small trees and bushes of the thicket carefully and head back to the vehicle. The only flaw in the plan was that they knew there were lions in the vicinity; they had heard contact calls earlier, and this was certainly 'lion grass'. With the sardonic words 'If you see a lion, *don't* tell me!', the lead guide turned towards the mountain and led out.

By this point it was starting to get dark so the group decided to stick to the mountainside and head straight back to the vehicle. It was a rough walk, exacerbated by the fact that the sun had set some time ago and the light was fading fast. This added the hazard of treacherous footing to a group of walkers who were, by then, in various stages of physical and emotional exhaustion. Many barked shins and semi-twisted ankles later, they were near to where they had left the vehicle. It was parked in a euphorbia thicket at the base of the mountain, and as they approached it in the gloom the sound of oxpeckers taking off alerted them to the presence of animals. Loading a cartridge into the breech of his rifle the guide said, 'Stay close behind me; if something comes toward us, anything at all, I'm going to shoot it.' Those last 40 metres back to the vehicle were really scary!

Safely back on the vehicle and driving out along the track Frank's wife commented that she'd been running so fast that her ears hurt from the wind. If she'd known where the vehicle was she would have beaten everyone to it!

This is an absolutely true story and it happened very early in Frank's career as a trails guide. He told me that the lessons that he learnt that day will remain with him for ever. He tells it to all his guides in training, and when I was one of these he told it to me too. Also, it represents another bitingly honest commentary on events that in hindsight would have been better avoided, indeed should have been better handled. I always believe that it reflects a very high level of honesty as well as insight when guides, or any other professionals come to that, remind us of their mistakes so that we are better informed and educated. I wish more doctors did it. I have repeated Frank's words here, word for word, for myself as a great reminder, and also for you to read the precise words of experience and wisdom handed down to those in the early stages of their guiding adventure:

1. Never start walking after midday. If things go wrong you don't have the luxury of considerable daylight to wait it out.
2. It is never a good idea to try to get closer to an animal if you already have a good view. This is especially important when you do not have a clear idea of exactly what you are approaching or how many of them might be there.
3. In certain circumstances running away while an animal is unsighted is an option.

In many countries across the world, the school run is part of many parents' daily routine. Come to think of it, increasingly these days a grandparental duty. I do it myself. For most of us it is nearly always straightforward and the only anxiety is whether heavy traffic may make you late. For a few parents, though, it may be very different.

Calum and Sophie McFarlane own and manage Lewa House, a delightful home and safari camp in the Lewa Conservation Area of Kenya. As with many other couples they share most of the childcare duties, notably the morning and afternoon school run so pivotal in the life of many families with young children. This is much the same as a school run anywhere else, miserable in the rain, time consuming and so on, but with some quirky extras such as getting stuck in the mud or being obstructed and delayed by an uncooperative herd of elephants.

The peaceful pool at Lewa. *(Maryann Williams)*

One May afternoon, it being his turn for this duty, Calum was waiting at the usual meeting point where another dad would drop off the two McFarlane children. The track junction where he was parked was in a thoroughly delightful piece of woodland protected from the otherwise inevitable depredations of elephants by a highly successful ecological scheme involving wire, electricity and an awful lot of money. He was a bit early and this offered a window of opportunity for some birding. So, armed with binoculars (he didn't take a rifle to pick up the kids) he hopped out of the vehicle and walked up the grassy track which, about 100 metres ahead, finished most pleasantly at a shaded, reed-fringed pool, the home of grosbeak weavers and an ever-changing cast of itinerant water birds. Perhaps the spoonbill would be there again.

Suddenly, somewhere in front, he heard a rustling noise. His first thought was 'buffalo'; not necessarily good news. But then out of some quite rich foliage came a lioness, walking with, it seemed, some intent. She growled and paced steadily towards him. Traditional weaponry had he none, but under pressure it's surprising what can be accomplished by judicious use of voice, arms and a pair of binoculars. Calum shouted and raised his binoculars above his head, making himself taller, trying to dominate. The lioness stopped and Calum began a slow retreat towards some trees; safety they were not but protection just a little. As he moved backwards the lioness came again, not an outright charge but definitely menacing. But he got to a tree and stood behind it, and as the lioness was now less sure of herself she stopped. This allowed a further slow retreat, from tree to tree, until his vehicle was within quick dash range. But don't run, he told himself, gently does it. And quickly into the car. She glared balefully at him for a while then turned and disappeared from sight.

I would love to know exactly what Calum said to his children and later his wife. But he didn't say.

12 MORE ABOUT CATS

I have included two stories from the same guide in this chapter. In some ways they are very similar but are both dramatic and, importantly, show very clearly how guides at the very top of the guiding tree are often extremely reflective in the retrospective analysis of a potentially serious confrontation with an animal.

It was the end of a long season; the days were getting longer and warmer and the guides more and more tired. This was one of those mornings when the guests were leaving early but, much to Phil Jeffery's disappointment, they insisted on doing a short morning walk; he'd have much preferred go out for a proper walk than bumble around close to camp, killing time. Phil is the part-owner and guide at a very beautiful camp in the Kafue National Park of Zambia and was already anticipating the huge workload that would hit him and his staff the moment the camp closed for the rainy season.

Anyway, on that morning he resigned himself to the inevitable, laced up his boots, completed his ritual morning coffee fix and set off on one of his favourite walks. An armed scout was in the lead, as is usual practice in Zambian National Parks, followed closely by himself directing the walk with two guests in tow. They were a delightful British couple with bush experience.

The particular walk he selected headed north, perpendicular to the trails of large breeding herds of elephant that drink at the nearby lagoon on a daily basis. Elephants approaching you are always something to watch out for so there was considerable advantage having such good visibility in the mixed woodland that they traversed. Termite mounds were dotted around and they offered both additional cover if it was needed and good vantage points. A bonus was that in the morning the wind had changed ever so slightly from its usual easterly direction and the party was heading into a quite heavy northerly breeze, ideal for getting closer to animals without being detected. Game trails criss-crossed their path and revealed the previous night's activities. There were signs of waterbuck, bush pig, common duiker and kudu, to name but a few. Overall a most pleasant stroll through open country, grass about calf length, accompanied by the ever-present sounds and smells of the bush. The cool early morning breeze on what promised to be another very hot day added to the feeling of contentment.

Suddenly Phil stopped dead in his tracks. He swiftly but quietly grabbed the scout's arm and turned to the guests, index finger pressed tightly to his lips. Everyone understood him immediately, but not even the scout with his rifle hanging loosely from his shoulder could see what Phil had seen. Right. Beneath. Their. Noses. Lying flat in the grass facing away from them was a beautiful, big leopard, perfectly camouflaged in the golden calf-length grass that they fought hard to protect from fire year after year. With his mind racing and everything seemingly frozen in time Phil's initial thought was that this must be a dead leopard … there is no way that they could have snuck up on this cryptic cat without it noticing; and so close! Surely the heavy human footsteps and voices would have alerted it to their presence? But no, it was breathing deeply and steadily, very much alive, but in a deep, deep sleep.

Leopards are lithe, powerful cats that have a seemingly sixth sense and, being solitary, are always acutely aware of their surroundings. Phil knew that it wouldn't take long before it would wake up and realise that it was under the scrutiny of some very wide eyes! But what to do? Any movement at all would have immediately alarmed the sleeping cat, and crouching down was not an option. When it saw them there must be no signs of weakness or intimidation as there could be only two outcomes at such close quarters – fight or flight! After what seemed like an eternity but what in reality was

In thick cover leopards aren't easy to see even when they are standing up. When lying down they can be near-invisible. *(Maryann Williams)*

probably a matter of a few short minutes, the leopard slowly woke up with the grace of an overfed house cat, rolled over onto its front and began to groom itself, licking its paws. Phil tensed, preparing himself for what might happen. The leopard stopped licking. Was something afoot? She looked over her shoulder, saw them and cocked her head to decipher what they were and what on earth they were doing so close. When she figured out what the statuesque figures were, she jumped up in a flash and like lightning was gone into the short grass. Then she slowed to a fast walk and looked over her shoulder once more before a sub-adult cub that we hadn't seen joined her and they disappeared amidst a trail of monkey and guineafowl alarm calls.

The party all let out an enormous sigh of relief. It had turned out to be a very positive once in a lifetime experience that none of them would ever forget. When the distances were paced out it was found that the leopard had been lying between 5 and 7 metres away from them. To add to the complexity of the encounter, in a nearby bush was the carcass of a recently killed puku which had clearly satiated the bellies of the two cryptic cats, putting them into a sort of food coma.

Phil says that they were lucky that day that the animals had an escape route. Although when given the chance animals will tend to avoid a physical confrontation, the ingredients were all there for what could have been a very different outcome; a kill, a cub, a fiercely protective mother, and a surprise encounter makes for a toxic mixture. Sometimes this happens and is unavoidable, but Phil felt that on reflection he might have been a tiny bit complacent. A short walk, fairly open country with good visibility, a bit tight on time, end of the season … Really good guides do this, learn from it and teach others about it to improve guiding standards. A walk is never too short or too quiet for anything to happen. Pay attention. Expect the unexpected.

Many of the activities in the early stages of Phil's company were centred either on the river or on foot, since he and his people sought out the remotest areas with no infrastructure. This was raw wilderness where wildlife was scarce and skittish, though everything was present, including poachers. Frequently they would assist the national parks with deployment of anti-poaching units (APU) to scour areas for illegal activities.

Early one afternoon the APU came back with nothing to report apart from a lone lioness in woodland not far from camp. Lions were seldom seen in those early days although they were heard frequently, and so Phil asked the team for the GPS location and any other clues they could offer him. He discussed the idea of an afternoon walk with the only guest in camp, a lady that he'd had the pleasure of guiding over the previous ten years at various places where he'd been lucky enough to work. She was keen to try find the lioness, and Phil certainly was.

Although the information given to Phil by the APU would be very helpful in starting them off, by now the lioness could be almost anywhere, near the camp or much farther away. But you have to start with a plan of sorts. After letting the camp know which direction they were headed, Phil briefed the accompanying scout and off they went. The reported location of the lioness had been entered into his GPS. He took the lead so he could follow the route on the GPS with the scout behind him and the guest close behind the scout.

It was late October and so very hot. Walking through the miombo woodlands with barely a breeze, beads of sweat dripped down their noses as they closed in on the GPS location. Phil turned off his radio in an attempt to be as quiet as possible but the carpet of fallen brachystegia pods crunched beneath their every step like cornflakes. Stealthy they were not! Despite having a presumptive location this was not going to be an easy find, and Phil considered the best approach would be to close in on the point in a tightening circle in the hope that they'd pick up some clues or even a glimpse of the lioness. In the hot, still afternoon, wind direction was not a consideration and in any case they were making more than enough noise for a lioness to hear them from a long way off. He figured that this would be no bad thing since where there was one lioness there was likely to be others and possibly cubs. A distant glimpse would be more than enough to make everyone happy!

The heat started to ease as the late afternoon sun dipped below the canopy of trees, spreading light in all directions and making it difficult to pick out shapes and movement. Aware that it was several kilometres back to camp Phil decided that it was time to turn back. Stepping to one side he broke rank to get his bearings on the GPS and decide the best route back. Then he looked up. Directly in front of him and with eyes locked on to his was an enormous male lion. He was just a dozen or so metres away, sitting on his haunches with teeth bared and tail flicking violently from side to side. In the same instant he let out a terrifying snarl and exploded into life tearing directly towards them through a thick stand of saplings. This was not the lioness they had been looking for.

In those days Phil carried a firearm, a BRNO CZ Magnum .375 to be precise, but the lion was so close and had charged without warning so there was no time to load, shoulder and fire a round, even if he had wanted to. It took just milliseconds for the lion to rush upon them, with his stiffened legs and upright posture accompanied by a ferocious noise. Phil raised the rifle above his head to make them appear a more formidable foe and with his right hand reached behind to grab the guest by her arm, shouting at the top of his lungs 'DON'T RUN! DON'T RUN! DON'T RUN!' The shouting was largely directed at the charging lion but also he had to ensure that nobody moved otherwise the episode might end very badly indeed. Fortunately the lion stopped just a few metres in front of them and a tense few moments followed as it decided whether to charge again or retreat. Phil fought desperately to override the natural instinct of running away. A brief glance over his shoulder reassured him that the scout, too, had stood firm. He could not attempt to load the rifle as any movement was agitating the lion further and in a single leap could have been on top of them.

But the lion suddenly, and a bit unexpectedly, took a few steps back, and Phil loudly (for the lion's benefit) discussed an exit strategy with the scout; they would gradually walk backwards with the scout leading the way, ensuring that they didn't trip over anything. Slowly they began to sidestep their way out of the situation. The first few tentative steps were accompanied by much growling and twitching which suggested another charge was imminent. They kept eye contact and slowly the lion calmed down. Eventually they reached a distance that the lion was comfortable with and he turned round back to the scrub from which he'd erupted. There he started feeding on something that looked like a warthog – even more reason for him to have been displeased with their arrival on the scene. It was a very quiet walk back to camp followed by a few stiff drinks.

In hindsight Phil speculated that the lion had seen them quite some time before the encounter and watched as they meandered around the woodland. Animals are acutely aware of being watched and since they clearly hadn't seen him, he had been quite content to lie low and wait for them to disappear. After all, almost always animals would far sooner avoid a physical confrontation given the chance. It had been pure misfortune that they had stopped right where he was. Phil wondered if the incident might have been avoided if he had kept his head up and had been scanning the middle distance rather than concentrating on the GPS and the end of his toes. Many guides would respond by saying that in relatively unknown terrain you will have to look at the GPS sometime. But as he says, it's a good reminder. Keep looking ahead.

Perhaps the last word here should be given to Carl Akeley (1864–1926), an African explorer, biologist, photographer and conservationist who said 'The lion is a gentleman – if allowed to go his own way unmolested, he will keep to his own path and will not encroach on yours.'

Sam Mopalo, a walking guide in Botswana, was working in the Okavango Delta guiding four guests whose main ambition was to 'walk dangerous animals'. This meant approaching them as closely as necessary to get a good view and/or a good photograph, all within the absolute rules of safety and not unduly disturbing the animals in question. The ideal of such a walk is that you accomplish this without the animal knowing that you are there at all. However, in the event this may not be possible, and just occasionally the approach becomes much more complex.

On night three of the guests' four-night stay, Sam was awakened by the sound of lions roaring. As he lifted his head from the pillow to check this out the roaring stopped. All he had was a general sense of its direction and, from its volume, an educated guess at the distance: about 5 kilometres he thought.

In the morning, after the customary rusk and coffee, the party drove for 5 kilometres in the approximate direction of the overnight roaring. They were six: four guests, Sam and his assistant guide. On reaching the area and rifle in hand, Sam led them in a wide circle from the vehicle to try and locate the lions by finding tracks and then following them. He was confident that they were in roughly the right place. They walked for some way through a lightly wooded area without finding any sign, and then emerged onto the open flood plain. Here was a world of cottonwool grass (*Imperata cylindrica*), standing about half a metre high with its characteristic white tops waving gently in the light breeze. Although cottonwool grass looks almost flat it is thick and high enough to offer concealment for a variety of animals. The other dramatic feature was that the plain was studded with termite mounds of varying sizes.

As they entered this very beautiful and typical delta landscape there was no sign or view of any animals. Not far in front of them was a particularly large and high termite

This lion has serious injuries from porcupine quills. One quill in the neck is making feeding very difficult. *(Donated anon)*

mound which Sam thought might provide an excellent viewpoint over the area, and it was towards this they walked. But the peace was abruptly broken by a dramatic and very persistent roaring, a lion surely, but where? It was very loud and presumably very close. Suddenly a lioness burst out from the grass and raced towards them. Sam chambered a round and aimed, shouting to his guest to freeze and stay behind him. He would take the charge if the lion kept coming and would have to shoot. But as she got closer he got the clear impression that she was going to stop. Her hind legs grew further apart and her forelegs were positioned more between them and stop she did, though very close, at about 10 metres. Her tail swished from side to side and the growling continued at high volume, now accompanied by snarling. It was a stressful time, a time that stretched out for five minutes, long enough for his rifle arm to get tired. Just when he thought she might try another run at him she stopped growling, turned and walked slowly away, just looking back to show her teeth and give them a farewell growl.

At this point Sam backed the guests away very cautiously until the lion was out of sight in the grass. Then, quickly back to the vehicle. Not out of necessity or because of a possible threat but to see if they could drive back, find her and observe her from the safety of a game drive vehicle. It might help solve the question of why she had been aggressive enough to give them the charge. So back they went and found her near the large termite mound and the explanation became clear. She had a kill and was defending it. Mind you, it was hardly a grandiose kill. Not exactly a large buffalo or even a tsessebe. It was Africa's largest rodent, a porcupine. It would weigh anything up to around 25 kilograms and would have been exceedingly difficult to kill because of the very sharp quills which can seriously damage lions, even lead to their death from infection. You have to ask whether it's worth it; the amount of meat is quite small compared with other options, and the energy expenditure, time taken and threat level is quite high. But maybe times had been hard for that lioness. Being a lion isn't easy.

Overall the guests had seemed to enjoy the experience. Being frightened and then safe very soon afterwards rarely has long-lasting adverse effects. They had wanted to get close to dangerous game on foot and unarguably had achieved that. But the assistant guide had been sufficiently alarmed to have an involuntary emptying of his bladder. Nobody laughed.

For me, the most fascinating thing was the lioness was relaxed and disinterested when they pitched up in the vehicle close to her. This, of course, is typical and reflects the habituation that frequent exposure to motor transport brings. On foot it's a different matter. Then humans are a threat to their offspring, their food or even their life. Going on foot into the wild has many attractions. For a lot of people the major attraction is to see and sometimes get close to animals. But it's easy to overlook the fact that this can bring with it a great deal of stress to the animals. The energy expenditure of a lioness charging is considerable, a significant percentage of the energy from the kill she's defending. We all need to think about that.

13 THE MOST DANGEROUS ANIMAL OF ALL

The phrase 'dangerous animals' summons images of lions, elephants, buffaloes and the rest of the Big Five plus a number of other suspects. It isn't always appreciated, though, that almost any animal encountered in the wild or even in some domestic scenarios might inflict significant harm. An unhappy illustration of this is a tragic event in 2015 that befell a 70-year-old man, Jimmy Robinson, at his home in the small town of Uitenhage in the Eastern Cape province of South Africa.

It was just after 8 p.m. on a January evening and dark outside when he and his daughter heard a great commotion outside his house. The noise was caused by his dogs, two Jack Russells, barking furiously. He left the house to investigate and was confronted by an extraordinary sight. One of the dogs was limping towards him, a hind leg clearly damaged in some way. The second dog was continuing to bark, challenging a beautiful and elegant antelope, a bushbuck bull, which was standing on the lawn. The bushbuck had slashed this second dog in the abdomen with one of its horns. During his attempt to ward off the bushbuck's attack on his dog, Mr Robinson was himself gored in the leg and fell to the ground. At that point the buck charged him again and this time inflicted a serious penetrating injury to his head as a result of which, some days later, Mr Robinson died. With horns up to 38 centimetres long, bushbuck are well known for being temperamental, occasionally aggressive and as a potentially formidable adversary. But the same may well be true for other horned antelopes when frightened or cornered.

The subject of which is *the* most dangerous animal in Africa often stirs up a rich debate. Buffalo, hippopotamus and elephant frequently top people's league tables in the risk stakes, crocodiles often get a mention but mostly people ignore the true top name on the leader board. Patricia Goodwin, a trails guide, has a very clear view as to which animal this should be and has recounted an incident which served to underline the opinion that she had held for many years.

The scenario was that a group of six walking guide students were coming to the end of a four-week course. This would, they hoped, be the first formal step on the road towards the qualification permitting them legally to lead guests on foot in a dangerous

Living in the bush during guide training on the night before this story.
(*Patricia Goodwin*)

game area. They were going on a three-night camp-out in the wilderness area of a national park. Not many people have the opportunity of experiencing this; there is something truly wonderful about sleeping out in the open in a wilderness area with little between you and potentially dangerous animals. The only things to disturb the starlit nights are an occasional lion roar or elephant trumpet, plus of course the mandatory turn at guard duty. For these students it was a fantastic opportunity to put into practice all that they had learnt, both in lecture room and bush, over the previous weeks.

It was around 6 a.m. on a cool autumn morning when they set out for the last of the morning walks. The summits of the hills were crystal clear against the sky, the light was good and there was really no wind at all. The party consisted of a lead and a back-up guide, both armed, and the six students. This was an exciting place to be: a mountainous area of the park, closed to the public and comparatively rarely visited. What a privilege to be allowed access to this wonderful area of natural beauty, just them and the wildlife.

They had been walking over quite rough terrain for a couple of hours, the sounds and that fresh scent of autumnal morning revealing itself as the sun rose, when they heard an odd but distant humming noise. Its source was much debated, but there was general agreement that in these conditions, especially in the hills, sound could carry a long way and it was probably traffic on a road outside the park or, possibly, near a lodge at the northern, quite distant, perimeter. In any case, just at that point they found fresh white rhino spoor that was manifestly more interesting than vehicle noises. The rhino was large, a bull. They might just be in business for a good encounter. Where was he going? Could they track him?

The tracks and some intelligent guesswork took the group up towards what Europeans called a col and Afrikaans colleagues a nek. And there he was. A grand and extremely large male white rhino. As so often up on the hills there was a bit of a breeze up there so, ably led by one of the students, they crept into some cover downwind of the animal to a position where they had a classic, textbook view of this magnificent beast. It was not just in the animal's comfort zone but in the students' as well. Photographs, smiles all round and, when they were satiated (though perhaps one can never have enough of views like that), a quiet and steady withdrawal back to the col. The continuation of the planned route lay down the shallow wide valley in front of them to a plain. All was well in their world and spirits were high, but hang on – what's that vehicle? It had been driven smartly along the track way down below them on the plain and stopped. Four camouflage-smocked figures jumped out, and the guides and students heard that classic sound of rifles being cocked. What on earth was going on? The figures fanned out and moved speedily upwards and towards the student group, occasionally disappearing into the ample cover provided by clumps of bushes and then reappearing, higher and closer. It looked awfully tactical.

They all froze. Stood really, really still. The lead guide, well-known locally and highly experienced, grouped everyone together and said, 'This is not good. Stay standing and don't move around. In fact don't move a muscle.' It was important in that context to ensure that the guides' weapons were in full view with butts grounded. Those guys meant business. Almost everyone proposed theories, all thinking it through quickly and carefully. Clearly it wasn't the army; they didn't operate here. Poachers mob-handed? No way. It was daylight, and anyway that's not how they do things. So it had to

Dressed to kill. The sniper in the anti-poaching unit. *(Patricia Goodwin)*

be the anti-poaching unit, the APU. They'd been known to shoot first and ask questions later. It could turn quite nasty if it wasn't handled right. One of the student guides was Patricia, who recorded the whole thing very carefully immediately afterwards. Later she said, 'I was 55 years old, the mother of three sons, and this was very definitely a situation I had never envisaged: the scariest encounter with any animal in any park in Africa so far, and the animal was human. I can't say that my life flashed before my eyes but there was definitely a flash photograph of my kids.'

All those thoughts, of course, took place over a very short time, probably just a few, very anxious, seconds. As the advancing uniformed group got closer, suddenly they were aware of two more guys coming up behind them, one in full ghillie suit; a sniper for goodness' sake. They all looked very tough and there were no smiles and no greeting. At least mildly encouraging was the fact that they weren't actually aiming the rifles at any of the students or the armed guides.

'Who are you, and what are you doing?' said a huge guy, the leader, very aggressively. 'We've being following you.' Aha, that explained the vehicle noise.

The leader of the student group explained very clearly, who they were and what they were doing, with heavy emphasis on the fact that they had permission from the parks board to be there, to do what they were doing, to carry weapons and so on.

'So where is the paper? I want to see the paper.'

There was no paper of course. This had been a telephone thing.

Predictably it got sorted out over the next few minutes. Radios buzzed, voices were raised in anger, blame suitably apportioned and peace broke out. But the APU guys seemed irritated on two levels. Firstly, they'd been messed around unnecessarily and denied 'intelligence information' as they put it. Secondly, Pat got the distinct impression that they'd been looking forward to an encounter with potential miscreants. After all, that's what they do. Their final riposte was to say in all seriousness 'Inside, we knew you wouldn't be poachers. You whiteys are rubbish poachers.' Bloody cheek.

So what did the student group learn, or be reminded of, from all this? Well, APUs really do exist; they're good at their job and they don't mess about. They're tough guys doing a tough and potentially dangerous job. More people should know about them. That's the good news. The bad news was that it had been derisively easy for communications to get, shall we say, confused. Of course this applies even if you're walking in a wilderness mountain area like the Drakensberg where there are no dangerous animals (barring the odd leopard and Lesotho dope smugglers) and no APU. You should tell everyone where you are going and what you are doing. And then tell them again. Also you should plan what you will do in a variety of dangerous circumstances though you can never predict them all.

The student group learned a big lesson from an event which could have turned out much more seriously. The Big Five are not the only dangerous animals out there!

Walking in the bush with guests and experiencing an actual confrontation with one or more poachers would be a very serious issue indeed. The first rule would be to get the hell out and the second, immediately following the first, tell somebody in authority as speedily as possible. Rarely, a different set of circumstances might pertain. For example,

Peter van Houdt.
(Peter van Houdt)

there are no guests, you are a long way from any communication facilities and you aren't certain about exactly what's going on – and there's nobody pointing a weapon at you. It can happen. A guide friend, Peter van Houdt, related this tale that took place in Botswana several years ago.

Peter had loved the Okavango Delta from the very beginning. No surprise, then, was his decision, many years after his first visit, to do his guide training there with Okavango Guiding School (OGS). The camp was in a superb area of bush some 55 kilometres from Maun.

On one very memorable day the student guides had set off early in two groups to do a long, 15-kilometre, training walk. The idea was to explore the bush, see what they would see and meet halfway from the two different start points so that they would all have transport to get back to camp at the end of the day. One group would take the vehicle, the other the boat, and swap for the return journey.

When Peter's group reached the halfway meeting point they were surprised to see two of the guys in the other group carrying a mopane pole with a dead white-backed vulture hanging from it. They'd found it on the trail and suspected it had been poisoned. It's common practice amongst poachers, when they've skinned and taken what meat they need from a carcass, to poison what's left. The poison is then ingested by vultures as well as jackals, hyaenas and other animals and they all die, thus not revealing any evidence of poaching by gathering near the spot and attracting unwanted curiosity.

A single dead vulture was a bit of a mystery, but both groups decided to follow their respective plans and so Peter and his team continued their walk. After an hour or more suddenly they heard a gunshot. The radio chattered in rather garbled fashion about a buffalo and gunshots, then promptly fell silent. What on earth was going on? They decided that on the basis of probabilities it was Grant Reed, the head of OGS and leading the other group, defending himself against an animal, possibly a buffalo. They were sorry to miss a piece of action like that – but, hey, there was always tomorrow.

Later, back at camp, it transpired that Grant had indeed needed to shoot a buffalo but not an old, grumpy dagha boy. It had been a lone youngish calf. Now that's downright unusual. Not just that it was a young female walking alone, but one prepared to give you the charge as well. There they all sat, 12 international and local Botswana student guides clustered around the campfire, considering whether there was any link between this and the presumed poaching activities. Had the buffalo been frightened by people with guns for example? Had its mother been shot? And what should be done about the possibility of poachers? If indeed there were any around. If they called out the authorities on a doubtful premise would they react? If they did it would take them some time to get people on the ground.

Ultimately it was decided that they should 'act responsibly' and re-visit the area on the following morning. They were well-armed so tolerably safe and had the vehicles to get through the still-high water, deep enough in one place for the water to come over the bonnet such that Peter rescued a couple of tilapia from the back seat when they reached terra firma.

They soon reached the suspect area, easily recognised by the presence of a large number of vultures, all crouched in the lower branches of the surrounding trees. Hopefully these ones hadn't eaten sufficient poison or simply hadn't died yet. The guys formed a sweep line, 12 metres apart, to search the area. The outline plan was to see if there were more dead birds and, if so, to collect them and burn them in order to remove the poison from the food chain. Amazingly, in no time at all they had collected 51 white-backed and white-headed vultures and three yellow-billed kites. It was a miserable business. But in spite of their big talk and the sharing out of five rifles they really hadn't taken seriously the possibility that the poachers might still be around.

Then a dog barked – but hang on, dogs weren't allowed in the area. This was a game-changer. Grant and Kenny, a local student guide, ran towards the noise and told Peter to keep the group safe whereupon he backtracked along their arrival route. A minute later they heard a gunshot, then a second, then two more and shortly afterwards a fifth. This was a bad moment. They had no idea what was going on.

Kenny suddenly appeared, running, out of breath, words spilling out. 'Grant wants the vehicle.' So Peter ran. Kenny ran with him. The two others with rifles stayed with the group. It was a long way back, much further than they remembered, well over a kilometre. As they ran Kenny, in short phrases as he was out of breath, explained the

The poisoned vultures collected by Peter and his group. *(Peter van Houdt)*

gunshots. Poachers often used donkeys to carry their illicitly gained meat out of the bush into town. Donkeys are good weight bearers, but crucially their tracks resemble those of zebras, which are much less likely to arouse unwanted curiosity. Grant had shot the donkeys, which would otherwise have run off, possibly to be rounded up and used again. This was a rather more dramatic version of the 'confiscation of proceeds of crime' system used in European and other courts.

During this frantic dash there was a jumble of thoughts racing through Peter's mind. Just four weeks ago he'd been a fairly normal, besuited management consultant, sitting comfortably in marble-floored offices, discussing with chief executives of large insurance companies and banks the business strategies which might be put in place to bring about changes within their organisations. Now, clad in not particularly clean bush gear, he was racing through the bush of the Okavango Delta, rifle in hand, to fetch a vehicle. This needed a reality check, but there was no time for that. They had to get there quickly. They did. And then was the first moment he had time to reflect on the situation.

As they drove back at far more than game drive speed Peter examined his soul. Did he want to be in this situation or not? That was easy. He was already there so had no choice. He was involved, like it or not. Whatever was going to happen, bring it on. When they got back to the group Grant was there. He climbed aboard and explained that they had indeed found the poachers' camp and that he had seen at least three of them running away. At this point Peter was sitting in the row immediately behind the driver, Kenny. He was armed and they were chasing armed poachers. He was high off the ground in an open-sided vehicle. A sitting duck. For a moment he contemplated lying down on the bench, but that wasn't his style. If there were poachers and they shot at him, he would shoot back. In a high-speed chase and with adrenaline coursing through the veins, legal implications about that sort of direct action are not at the forefront of the brain. The chase, the hunt, the anger, all take over.

They raced around a thicket of tall and sturdy trees and saw, directly in front, a huge cloud of dust in the air. They stopped. A pause for thought. It wasn't the direction in which the poachers had fled, but they could have turned. So into the dust they drove but it was a different and rather less dangerous animal they found – a herd of buffalo, probably spooked by gunshots or the poachers or whatever. They saw nothing of fleeing men, and returned to the remainder of the party still on foot.

Together they analysed the situation and came up with a plan. First they would collect the remaining vultures and burn them. So a team of people started to do just that. It was a very miserable business, heartbreaking even. Then they would revisit the poachers' camp and document everything. If they could gather sufficient evidence to support a prosecution it would be a job well done. Ideally they would have returned to their base and contacted the Botswana Defence Force (BDF) though whilst the military were making their way to the area the poachers might well come back, take everything they could and wreck the crime scene. That was too big a risk to take. Everyone agreed that they would be prepared to be involved in legal proceedings and appear as witnesses if required.

When they reached the camp it looked as if the poachers had been living there for at least a couple of weeks. It appeared that they'd bugged out as soon as the dog had barked so almost certainly they knew other people were around. All their stuff was lying about: water bottles with names on, other personal items, a branding iron and lots of meat including a giraffe and a buffalo carcass. Crucially there was a poison container with what looked like good fingerprints on it. They put everything that looked important into a plastic bag and took many, many photographs including images of their tracks. Having burned the dead birds they took everything back to their camp and informed the authorities.

The next day the BDF anti-poaching people came and were taken to the scene. They took possession of the evidence that had been collected and copies of the photographs as well as statements from a number of people. Later forensic examination of samples of the carcasses, the poison container and the meat from the crop of one of the dead vultures proved that in each case the poison was identical. With the names of the poachers available it was easy to apprehend two of them and match their fingerprints both with those found on their personal belongings and on the poison container. In due course both were sentenced to 10 years imprisonment. They never learned what happened to the third man.

The memory that lives with Peter was not the great news of the criminals being caught. It was the image of all those dead animals and a group of grown men with tears in their eyes surveying the carnage. This wasn't some dirt-poor guy taking an impala for the pot. This was organised crime for big money, the bushmeat trade. Indeed, even if you could excuse the killing you could never justify poisoning. With carcasses left lying about, poison will eventually spread right through the food chain. Locally it would be disastrous. In the final analysis, in spite of the sadness, Peter felt they had done a good job: they'd contributed. Also it was, without doubt, an educational experience – though not necessarily what he'd thought he was signing up for. Now he knows that it's just part, a necessary part, of being a field guide.

There is an important footnote. On 20 June 2019, Botswana's Department of Wildlife and National Parks announced that they had identified a mass poisoning site in a former hunting area close to the Botswana–Zimbabwe border. Three elephants had been killed by poachers and the carcasses then laced with poison. This, as described in the story above, was an attempt to hide the poaching site from the anti-poaching personnel by reducing the number of vultures that would otherwise be flying around or roosting at the site and thus acting as a clue to the event. No less than 537 dead white-backed, hooded, white-headed, lappet-faced and cape vultures were dead at the scene as well as 2 tawny eagles. Worse, this was within the breeding season, which was likely to increase the number of victims substantially through the loss of chicks and eggs. These vultures, who provide an invaluable service to the ecosystem by cleaning up carcasses and thus reducing the spread of disease, are already classified as 'endangered' or 'critically endangered'. The incident ranked as a near-catastrophe for vultures in the area.

14 SOME SPECIAL INSIGHTS

The guide Kane Motswana appeared in Chapter 8. As a child he had lived in a small settlement called Gudigwa in the north-west of Botswana on the edge of the Okavango Delta. The families there were all hunter-gatherers who relied absolutely on the bush and the river for their food. They spoke the Bukakhwe San language. Kane told me a story from his early childhood that gives us considerable insight into the early bush education that underpinned his subsequent success as a guide.

Then aged 9, Kane was out in the bush hunting with his dog, Xqhaonxai (the pronunciation is difficult!), reputed to be the best hunting dog they had. He was part of a party that included his father and several other men, including cousins and uncles. Together they numbered 15. They were hunting for buffalo, eland, kudu, warthogs and impala. This was traditional legal and licensed hunting using spears and bows and arrows. Primarily they were searching for food but they would make use of the skins of the animals as well.

At 6 p.m. and about 30 kilometres from home, Kane and Xqhaonxai were out at the front of the group when he received a verbal message that his father, who was near the back of the group, had been taken extremely ill. He hurried back to his dad though he recalls that his main anxiety and disappointment at the time was that the dog carried on the hunt without him. What he found when he reached his father was profoundly worrying. He was complaining of severe pain in his chest, bad headache and extreme tiredness. He had a high fever as well. His father, who Kane called 'Mbaa', was very angry that the other members of the party had gone on ahead without them but decided that the two of them should walk slowly to an open area by a waterhole. By then it was dark so Kane had to follow the tracks of the other members of the party to find it. It was a difficult journey. His father had to stop every 200 metres to rest, but eventually they made it. Apart from a water supply there were places to rest though many people had died there, mostly killed by lions. They would need to be very watchful.

Then the body blow. Kane's dad told him that he was now a man and would need to think about how to save himself when he died later on that night. This must have been a terrible moment for the young lad who, it must be remembered, was still not ten years old. At first light, he was told, he must follow the tracks made by the other members of the hunt, and this process would certainly lead him home. On arrival there he must tell his mother that he, his father, was dead and she would need to retrieve the body. 'You mustn't,' he said, 'be worried about me. Death is just a normal thing – but you, my son, must save yourself. You can look after me during the night but you must also sleep. You'll be fine.'

Kane built a fire and cooked some meat they'd brought along as well as fetching water to drink and to bathe his father, who still had a high fever. He was very frightened and in equal measure desperately worried that his beloved father might die and appalled by the thought that he would be on his own in the bush a long way from home.

It was at this point that Kane's father decided to talk to his Ngoritsere, his fortune-telling stick, made from the silver terminalia or silver cluster-leaf tree. His father was well-known as a fortune teller and much revered amongst his people. He asked the stick specific questions. Would there be any predators visiting the waterhole this night? 'No' said the stick. Would there be *any* significant animals? 'Yes,' said the stick, 'elephants will come.' Good news indeed, but his father, a wise man, pointed out that although the stick didn't tell lies, sometimes it got things wrong. He thought 90 per cent accuracy was a fair estimate. Kane kept the fire going all night as well as attending to his father. No lions disturbed them, but sure enough, in the middle of the night a large group of elephants came to drink at the waterhole.

In the morning, much to Kane's relief, his father was a little better. So they set off, father and son together, following the tracks that would lead them to safety. Meanwhile, back at their village Kane's mother had heard that the other men had left her son and her husband alone in the bush. Understandably she was absolutely furious with the men and immediately set out, backtracking the main party's spoor, and met Kane and his father about halfway to the waterhole. They returned to the village together. This is how you grow up in the bush.

The Face at the Window

The startling nature of this deserves a thriller title! The Balule Private Nature Reserve is a particularly nice area of bush lying to the west of the world-renowned Kruger National Park, a little way south-west of the town of Phalaborwa and referred to briefly in Chapter 7. Importantly, it has open borders with the Kruger and is part of the same ecosystem with the highly attractive River Olifants forming its eastern border. It is, therefore, Big Five country. This is where I did my initial guide training, under the mentorship of the highly experienced guide Ian Owtram. He, however, makes only a minor appearance in this saga and the starring rôle is taken by his wife Mel, a field guide in her own right. Although most of the events described in this book are related to walking in the bush, living in the bush presents many of the same challenges, and this story recounts something of a twist in the usual tales.

It was 3 a.m. when the noise woke Mel from a deep sleep, an easy time to be puzzled by off-stage sound effects. It was a very loud banging and crashing. And was that heavy breathing she could hear? It was difficult to make out what it might be. But the family lived in the bush, a dangerous game area with no fences, so there were endless possibilities. Not that long ago, in the middle of the night some elephants had dug up the water supply for goodness' sake. Anyway, on this occasion Ian was away so she lay there listening for a while until the house shook after a particularly violent roaring sound. So it was a lion. Generally that wouldn't be a problem because that's what you hear in the bush. But he sounded awfully close so Mel decided that this required investigation.

She walked through the house without putting the lights on. There was nothing obviously untoward. The outside light didn't give any clues either, though Mel had wondered if the animal was up away from the house where their vehicles were parked. The office window might offer a better view, so she leaned across the desk and had just started to open the venetian blinds when 'CRASH!' a lion's bloody face smashed against the glass with a loud roar. It was like one of those scenes in a film designed to make the audience jump. And Mel did. She fled out of the room, closing the door behind her, heart pounding. She grabbed the two children from their rooms, one of which had open windows, with a serious predator outside, put them into her own bed and promptly joined them.

Next she rang Ian, who was some distance away at a meeting, and after reassuring him that there was no serious medical problem with her or the children, explained the lion situation. All he said was, 'Oh no, I'm missing all the excitement!' Typical husband response, she thought. But at least he agreed that some moral support would have been nice, and suggested she should stay in bed until morning, then phone the reserve ranger, Pieter Pretorius. So she lay there, listening to crunching and munching and more banging: clearly the lion had a kill. Understandably, sleep was impossible and so, to pass the time and by way of distraction, she picked up a book she'd been reading and opened it precisely at the page where a voracious lion was making a kill. That wouldn't do. Mills & Boone turned out to be a much better option. After about an hour but still before sunrise everything went quiet. There was no way that Mel was going to get any more sleep and so she just lay there, wondering what the lion was doing and, more anxiously, where he was.

When the sun was up they all got out of bed. Now was the time to look around inside the house and try and tease out exactly what had been going on. Her instructions to the kids were very clear. 'Stay here in the bedroom and whatever you hear or see, don't move. Just stay here. Right here, with the door shut.' The first pressing question was could the lion possibly have broken the window and actually be in the house? Perhaps lying peacefully asleep on the desk in the study? Mel left the bedroom, closed the door and crept along the passage, stooping to peer through the keyhole of the study door. Nothing. No lion. The window looked intact, so she risked further exploration. No opening the blinds this time but she went to one side of the window and squinted down the side of the blinds. There was a yellow mass of some kind on the ground just outside. It might well be the lion sleeping at the scene of the crime. But it wasn't a great view, so she repeated the trick on the other side of the window and solved the problem. The yellow mass – or, more accurate, mess – was stomach contents, and there was a trail of blood leading from it and up over a small wall. So the incident probably now was resolved and the family could get into its usual routine.

This routine included use of the car and so, after telling the children what was happening and making breakfast, Mel telephoned Pieter, who advised staying inside until he came round. Soon afterwards he arrived, parked near their own vehicles and got out of his. Immediately, a lion, *the* lion one supposed, a young male, stood up in nearby long grass and roared at him. He got back in the car with some dispatch and let the animal calm down. The lion was swishing his tail from side to side, ears pinned back, and seemed distinctly unimpressed with the new arrival. After a few more equally unsuccessful attempts, Pieter drove to the other end of the house, where he was out of sight of the beast. Then he went out into the garden to check on the lion's behaviour and the latter, eventually recognising force majeure, fussed about a bit before dragging the remains of the kill deeper into the bushes. Mel needed to get her game drive vehicle, which was not far from the lion, so they drove back around the house to it and parked behind it. But every time there was an attempt to get out of Pieter's car and into the game drive vehicle the lion roared from the bushes with ears back and tail swishing, though eventually he just walked away. That night there were hyaenas all around.

When Ian returned two days later they explored the area around the house. The most dramatic finding was a beautifully clear print of the lion's bloody nose on the low window of the study. Underneath that were scratch marks from the vigorous defence put up by the prey, a female waterbuck. Indeed, it was this mighty fight that had caused such a commotion, kicking and thrashing against the house. A larger animal such as a male of the same species might well have broken the window with its horns. There were trails of blood everywhere. But the quirkiest finding was a child's wheelbarrow lying underneath the entrails, bloodied and bashed about. It was this, completely caught up in the mêlée, that had been banging against the wall to such effect.

Mel had seen a lot whilst living in the bush and she is, after all, a qualified guide. But the nature of this incident, especially being alone with our small

Mel's lion, brilliantly camouflaged, taken the following morning.
(Mel Owtram)

children, made her very wary of using the office at night for some considerable time. As she said to me a long time after the event, 'If I try, I can still hear and see him.'

> Things that go 'bump' in the night
> Should not really give one a fright.
> It's the hole in each ear
> that lets in the fear.
> That and the absence of light!
>
> Spike Milligan (1918–2002)

WHAT DOES A TERMITE LOOK LIKE?

Although this book has been almost entirely about walking in dangerous game areas, from time to time I have come across stories that just cry out to be recorded. The first of these is one of the funniest guiding tales I have heard, all the funnier because it arose from readily understandable tourist innocence. For those who are unfamiliar with termites, essentially they are small, pale soft-bodied insects up to 1 centimetre in length who live in huge colonies. Over 3,000 species have been identified.

Sam Mopalo is the Maun-born Botswana field guide who we met in Chapter 12. He had been contracted to meet a tourist couple at a nearby airstrip. As they were Japanese, there had been some concern about language and understanding, but Sam was greatly relieved when he met them; their English was excellent. It was to be their first visit to the bush.

A large termite mound. The hole at the base has been excavated by an Aardvark, an insectivorous animal that is particularly fond of termites. *(Jeff Williams)*

A warthog emerges from an aardvark hole. *(Maryann Williams)*

It's well known that tourists take a lot of photographs, sometimes on an industrial scale. This couple was no exception. From the moment they arrived in the bush their cameras were active. Every time they passed a group of impala Sam had to stop the vehicle: click, click, click. Then there came the moment when they saw their first termite mound. 'Stop!' they shouted. 'What is that?' 'It's a termite mound,' answered Sam, 'a place where termites live.' 'Aha!' they cried, and took a number of photographs. At the next termite mound again they called for a halt. More photographs. At the third Sam once more was required to stop. But this one was different. In its broad base and facing the track was a large, old aardvark burrow. The vehicle brakes squealed as it stopped, and the couple armed and pointed their cameras.

Suddenly, from the hole burst a large and heavily tusked male warthog. 'Termite!' they shouted, cameras clicking furiously, 'termite, termite, termite!'

MATING CALLS

As a preface to the next story some background information may be helpful for less experienced bush visitors. The lion's roar is the most impressive sound made by any cat. Although it can be just a single loud roar of threat, typical roars consist of 30–60-second or longer bursts of vocalisations that can be divided into three phases. The 'intro' consists of low-intensity moans that gradually morph into the second

The boma at Sausage Tree Safari Lodge. (*Sausage Tree Safari Lodge*)

phase – more obvious roars that increase in intensity and duration and build up towards a climax, shortening in duration just before the peak. The third and final phase, the 'outro', comprises a sequence of grunts. Probably this sequence represents a contact call, made by males or females, between single or groups of lions separated by a distance.

It was a balmy evening in a safari camp within the Greater Kruger National Park and the surrounding bush was quiet. Around 9 p.m. the evening meal was well under way in the boma,[9] hosted by Sonja, one of the owners. The main course had just been cleared and the guests, their tables grouped around the central fire, were chatting quietly as they awaited dessert.

Suddenly Sonja heard the oh-so-familiar noise of big cat communication. Finger pointed at the sky, he said urgently, 'Listen, listen, everybody. Shhhhh. Lions, and they're not far away.' Everyone stopped talking. They all listened carefully. Then, after a few seconds, one couple started looking at each other. Slightly awkward glances were exchanged; after all it's impolite, even difficult, especially on a technical matter, to contradict not just the owner of the property but someone who spends their life in the bush. Preceded by a slight and apologetic cough, one of the guests said, 'It's not lions.'

---

9 Thorny stockade, sometimes used as a livestock enclosure, and also (as in this case) used as a protective barrier for an encampment in the wilderness, or to enclose an area with a central fire.

There followed a long pause as recognition of the source of the sounds dawned amongst the diners. The oriental couple in Tent 4, adjacent to the boma, had excused themselves from dinner, saying they were very tired. They were on their honeymoon. Almost immediately the dessert arrived and the conversation resumed, though possibly a little louder than before.

Even experts make mistakes from time to time.

15 INTO THE FUTURE

We know that there has been a massive decline in the global insect population. A review in the highly respected journal, *Biological Conservation,* in 2019 suggested that 40 per cent of the world's insect species are likely to be extinct in the next few decades. The main drivers of this are habitat loss due to intensive agriculture and agrochemical pollutants. The implications of these statistics make discussions about large animal losses in Africa almost pale into significance. However, these animal problems are another symptom of the same worldwide affliction that threatens our natural habitats – and, ultimately, theoretically at least, human survival. This, the final chapter of the book, starts by considering some of the dramatic changes in animal population that are likely to affect guides and their guests in their enjoyment of the African bush within the next few decades. Essentially, it is quite possible that some species considerably larger than insects will disappear from the wild completely. Walking in the bush 50 years from now, assuming that there will be sufficient residual bush to walk in, may make for a rather different and possibly less rewarding safari than it can be now.

14 November 2013. A Thursday. A calm and pleasantly warm morning. The lead guide was Frank Bouwer, and we were a mixed group of qualified walking guides and trainees. It had been an auspicious beginning to a bush walk, for within 15 minutes we had found a leopard perched on a rock right in front of us. Then we found a comfortable seated viewing platform amongst some rocks to watch a herd of buffalo parade below us.

Just before we moved off this vantage point we espied a lone brown hyaena clearly on a mission. It was looking neither left nor right, head up and down repeatedly, presumably on a scent. Interesting. So we followed. We gained height gradually up a small valley through thick bushes to emerge on an open plateau above. At that point we ran into a veritable wall of an appalling smell. A kill, surely. That's what the hyaena had recognised. Indeed it had now almost disappeared into some scrub, though we could see glimpses of it fussing around something. So no lions here; they wouldn't have tolerated a lone hyaena. Nevertheless we approached very cautiously. Trying to

Early in the walk, a buffalo parade from our gallery seat. *(Jeff Williams)*

The dreadful moment of finding the first of the two poached rhinos.
The horn has been removed with a saw. *(Jeff Williams)*

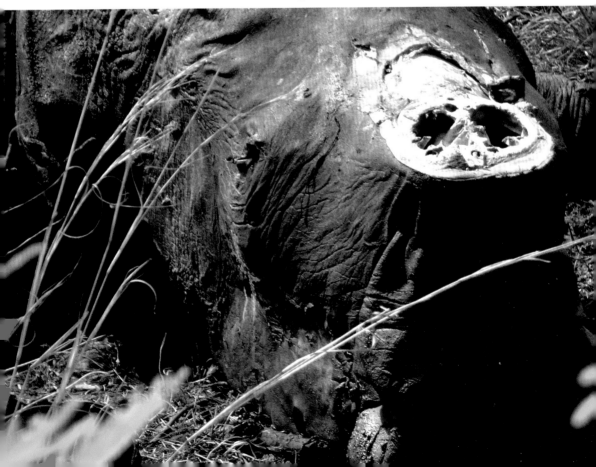

avoid surprises is always a good plan. But then we got a clear visual of the scene. It was devastating. There in front of us was a dead white rhinoceros. Not just dead but killed by poachers. Its horns had been removed, probably with an electric saw. Just 50 metres away lay another.

Few of us had witnessed this before except in photographs. We were all upset. And angry. Very angry. So angry that Frank, our leader, didn't feel able to continue leading, fearing that he wouldn't be able to concentrate sufficiently for safety. He handed over to his back-up guide and called the authorities on his mobile phone. The following day we all went on an anti-poaching patrol, still very fired up. It was a good job we didn't come across any poachers.

The rhino's greatest misfortune is that he carries a fortune on his nose.

Lee M. Talbot (1959)

Both white and black rhinos were widespread and abundant until Europeans arrived in the 17th century. Subsequently, white hunters systematically virtually wiped out both populations, with some claiming bags of over a thousand each. Most of this was simply for sport and for trophies. Rhino horn had no currency at that time. By 1892 the white rhino (*Ceratotherium simum*) was considered probably extinct in South Africa but a number, less than 100, survived the slaughter and remained in the iMfolozi

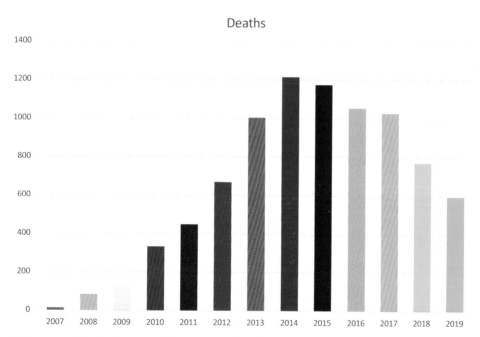

Rhinoceros deaths from poaching in South Africa.

area. This was the saviour of the animal. Subsequently the pressure on the animals was more related to the inevitable and insatiable demands of an increasing human population for living and farming land, thus limiting the rhinoceros to the more secure environment of national parks, nature reserves and other similar private areas.

More recently another rhino population catastrophe has burst upon the scene, this time driven largely by poaching to satisfy the apparently limitless demand for rhino horn for use in the Chinese and Vietnamese traditional medicine market. There has also been pressure to supply the same raw material for ceremonial daggers in the Yemen, though this is not on the same scale.

Between 1970 and 1992 the black rhino population fell by 96 per cent. In 1970 the estimated number in Africa was approximately 65,000, but by 1993, after a major poaching onslaught, only 2,300 remained. There was then some recovery but, particularly in South Africa, renewed carnage after 2008 has led to a catastrophic loss of both white and black rhinoceros. The statistics are stark. In South Africa over the 10-year period between 2007 and 2016, well over 6,000 rhinos were poached. Particularly for 2018 and 2019 the declining numbers of rhinos being poached looks encouraging. But it should be borne in mind that this is against a background of many fewer remaining rhino.

Elephant poaching for ivory is an ever-present threat, and has been for over a century. In 1900 a reliable estimate of African elephant numbers was somewhere above

African elephant population since 1900.

10 million. The 20th century saw sport hunting, legal hunting for ivory, poaching and increasing land requirements for a rapidly expanding population reduce the number by at least 95 per cent. Quantifying the 21st-century decline is tricky. It is suggested that between 2006 and 2015 over 100,000 elephants were killed, and the World Wildlife Fund estimate that over 400,000 wild elephants remained in the Africa of 2018. However, the statistics quoted by different organisations are often contradictory. What is certain is that poaching continues continent-wide, and there has been a recent upsurge in poaching and illegal ivory trafficking. In 2018, over a period of a few weeks, in the hitherto elephant safe haven of Botswana well over 70 carcasses were discovered, mostly of large bulls. This type of incident probably is driven by increasing demand in Asia. Currently China has the largest consumer market in the world for ivory ornaments and jewellery.

Although stories in this book illustrate the potential risk to humans, these are undoubtedly dangerous times for lions. In the Africa of the early part of the 19th century, wherever conditions were suitable you found lions. For example, until 1910 Morocco had a decently large population, and much the same applied to Algeria where lions occurred in such numbers that the then French colonial administration paid a bounty for every animal destroyed. In the early 20th century British Somaliland, since 1960 part of the independent country of Somalia, was one of the most famous lion countries of Africa, and they were still numerous in some inland areas in the 1950s. But unhappily, in this, the 21st, century, there are few lions north of a line drawn through Kenya. Much of this loss of lion populations throughout Africa is a result of the so-called human–wildlife conflict, in essence loss of suitable habitat because of the often necessary thirst for agricultural land. Overall there has been a 40 per cent reduction in lion numbers over the last 20 years or so.

Additionally, there is the recent massive escalation of the trade in animal body parts, not just the well-known trade in elephant ivory and rhinoceros horn, but affecting tens of thousands of species. A recent study by the Born Free Foundation revealed a startling breadth of use of various parts of lions. These included their fat for back and joint pain, skin and lungs for whooping cough, liver for headaches and veins for erectile dysfunction. Prominent amongst these was the wearing of pieces of skin, whole paws or any small bone around the neck or waist as a talisman to ward off spiritual attack and to confer the 'strength of a lion' to the user. Animal products have long been used in African traditional medicine as well as in other parts of the world.

I have no enthusiasm whatsoever for professional lion hunting. However, it adds only a very small percentage of risk to the future existence of lions, relying as it does largely on animals bred in captivity. But there remains well publicised truly wild lion hunting in the various parts of southern and eastern Africa where hunting is still legal.

It's not only dangerous animals that suffer from human predation. Often described as the gentle giants of the savanna, giraffes are creeping towards extinction without much recognition. Since 1990 there has been a decline of about 40 per cent in giraffe numbers. As usual, habitat loss is important, but illegal hunting for the bushmeat trade also plays a part. Less visible are giraffe parts obtained by trophy hunting, and there is particularly good evidence of American trophy hunters supplying the US market with many giraffe parts including bones and skin. Presently this is not illegal. Examples of sales items from giraffes include leather covers for bibles, leather boots, whole skins, hide pillows, hide bar-stools, bone pistol grips and tail-hair bracelets. There is even a market for giraffe eyelashes. Some sellers claim that their products all originate from giraffes killed to save African villages from aggressive herds of giraffe threatening loss of life. That really is a preposterous statement.

Much further down the league table in size is the extraordinary but massively endangered pangolin. This solitary, scaly and nocturnal mammal, also known as the scaly anteater, lives on termites and ants. It has been termed the least known, most hunted and most trafficked animal in the world. Four of the world's pangolin species live in Africa. Although almost all of their body parts are used, they are mainly poached for their scales and meat. The scales have a wide range of traditional medicinal uses throughout Asian and African cultures, though it is demand from China that is believed to be driving most of the global trade. In China and Vietnam the meat is considered a delicacy. It is estimated that one million pangolins have been poached since 2000.

Poaching and its prevention is a complex problem almost invariably driven by a toxic combination of, on the one hand, greed and on the other hand abject poverty. The latter tends to be the lot of the perpetrator on the ground, often very poor but with excellent bush and sometimes military skills, who is the most likely to be apprehended. Greed is largely the motive of the higher echelon controllers of

One of the answers? A de-horned rhino in South Africa.*(Rob Guerton)*

the business, the Mr Bigs, who are rarely caught and, when they are, have sufficient wealth and sometimes connections to avoid the full weight of the law. Presently, insufficient anti-poaching forces, weak law enforcement and local and national political corruption together make for an arena of poor prevention in many, if not most, of the affected countries.

As I write this I am aware of the considerable volume of support worldwide for any action which might mitigate what is presently a veritable carnage. There is a particular emphasis on the rhinoceros situation. Recently I had the opportunity of visiting a reserve in Africa where there has been considerable success in anti-poaching measures. The success seems to have hinged on two specific initiatives. The first involved stringent electronic supervision of all the game rangers whose numbers had been increased dramatically, operating in randomly selected pairs on an absolutely prescribed route itself unknown until they set out. The second was the creation of a highly motivated 'intelligence service' whose members watched and listened in all centres of population surrounding the reserve. Both of these operations were fuelled by considerable finance from an international source, and therein lies an important issue. Although I understand the pressure to de-horn rhinos, identify them by DNA profile or other tactics, at the end of the day it's money that talks. More money and more high-profile political will is going to make all the difference.

After a discussion about the dangers to animals it's an easy leap to considering the likelihood of dangers to those who walk in the bush, be they guests or the guides themselves. Having read some or all of these tales you might reasonably ask if the risks can be quantified. The quick answer is that it is impossible to give any precise answer, for there are almost no statistics. The only published study of the risks posed by wild animals to tourists in South Africa examined newspaper reports. The authors found that between January 1988 and December 1997, seven tourists were killed and fourteen injured by wild animals. Of these twenty-one incidents only three occurred on organised walks – presumably, though not certainly, led by an appropriately qualified guide. None of the three proved fatal. Two of the reports clearly describe the sort of extraordinary behaviour that carries an inevitability of an adverse, indeed fatal, outcome. For example, notwithstanding the clear notices prominently displayed, two visitors to a lion park near Johannesburg left their vehicle to pose for photographs using a nearby pride of lions as a background. In the second case, at a different reserve, a young man left his vehicle and walked 30 metres towards a pride of lions.

To supplement this published report, during the preparation of this book I did an internet search of the media for the subsequent 15-year period – that is, from January 1998 to December 2013 – covering southern and eastern Africa, including Zambia. This turned up twenty-four incidents, two thirds of which involved elephants. Nine were guided walks and all nine had experienced an elephant encounter, with six

The joy of walking in the bush. The author with a group of Motsumi Bush Course Apprentice Guides in Pilanesberg National Park. *(Patricia Goodwin)*

fatalities, one of which was a guide. It would be a mistake to assume that either of these forays into the written and electronic literature tell the whole story. Probably most of the fatal incidents will be captured, but an unquantifiable number of the non-fatal will be missed. Nevertheless, it does offer a glimpse into the issue.

Walking in the bush with a safari guide is extraordinarily safe. There is little to match the first time you stand, emotionally naked, modestly close to a huge bull elephant who stares at you and then turns his head to continue eating, having considered the matter and deemed you unimportant. Or to creep quietly using every piece of available cover to get 20 metres from a heavyweight male white rhino who never sees, never hears and never smells you, before you move away just as quietly without him knowing you were ever there. This safety aspect is hugely important. It is the guests who enjoy walking and driving in the bush that are likely to be conservation's key ambassadors. They will have at least as much and possibly more influence than wildlife charities or celebrities, because their experience will have been so much more personal. So ensuring not just their enjoyment but also their safety becomes paramount. Let's be clear. Many, many guides go right through their career, whatever length it is, without a truly life-threatening incident, and only a tiny number of guides have had to shoot an animal.

Although the problems of available land, poaching and so on are very real threats to wildlife and thus to safaris (the commonly used word derived directly from the Swahili word meaning 'journey'), it would be both unfortunate and inappropriate to finish on a downbeat note, for there is plenty to be optimistic about. The first regular, organised, professionally led walks in the South African bush started in March 1959, pioneered by the iconic Ian Player and called Wilderness Trails; they were operated in the Umfolozi[10] Game Reserve. Since then there has been a veritable explosion of walking trails in dangerous game areas throughout southern and eastern Africa. In South Africa alone there are probably hundreds each day. Alongside this lies the undoubted improvement in guide training and skills development that has occurred in all the relevant countries. Clearly defined standards are commonplace, practical assessments the norm, and often grading systems have been put in place to reward higher achievers. Compared with the knowledge base as well as the professional and communication skills that we tourists often experienced 20 years ago, the standard of guiding today is incomparable. No longer does it require large mammal sightings to make a walk both fascinating and memorable. These days guides have an in-depth knowledge of so many other aspects of wildlife to demonstrate to their guests varying from the excitement of inducing antlion larvae to show off their ambush tactics, to the discovery of a fantastically disguised nightjar egg lying almost under your feet or the identification of the weeping wattle tree (*Peltoforum africanum*) whose feathery leaves can be used as emergency bush toilet paper. A treasure trove of the African natural world awaits the explorer on foot in the bush.

As I am a 'hobbyist' guide, my respect and admiration knows no bounds for those professional walking guides who take guests out on a daily basis to experience the wonders of the African bush. As these stories illustrate, walking in the bush, however informative, stimulating and exciting, takes high-quality guiding to provide a great and yet safe experience.

---

10 Now joined with Hluhluwe to form Hluhluwe-iMfolozi Game Reserve.

The Contributors

Owen Booysen has been a professional safari guide for 10 years and runs his own safari company, Chui Safaris.

Frank Bouwer was born in Kenya to Dutch and Welsh parents. He describes himself as a professional adventurer, having worked as soldier, policeman, commercial fisherman, professional hunter, field guide and hot air balloon pilot.

He has been guiding since 1999 and is FGASA Level 3 SKS (DA) qualified and a FGASA assessor. Recently, as well as flying, he was field operations manager for Mankwe Gametrackers at Pilanesberg NP and focused more on mentoring aspirant trails guides than on guiding clients. Now he lives with his wife in Australia and pilots balloons. Up, up and away, Frank!

Liam Burrough is a is a FGASA Lead Trails guide at Ulusabi in the Sabi Sands area of the Kruger National Park.

James Carne is a FGASA Lead Trails Guide. An Englishman, he has no regrets about having decided to live in South Africa, as he met his lovely wife Sonja there. Together they built their dream small, luxurious and intimate tented camp, Sausage Tree, in the Greater Kruger National Park.

Jo Cooper specialises in tours throughout Africa and describes himself as just a happy guy who loves his continent and has been lucky enough to have made a career out of that love!

'I'm always looking for the next adventure, come join me sometime :) at Footsteps Through Africa.'

Calvin Cottar is one of East Africa's most renowned private guides and part of family that has been running safaris in Kenya for 90 years. In addition to being a private guide, Calvin and his wife Louise also have a permanent tented camp, Cottar's 1920s Safari Camp, situated within a 6,000-acre private conservancy and less than a mile from the Maasai Mara game reserve.

Greg Esterhuysen is a senior field guide working for Mankwe Gametrackers, and has worked in the Pilanesberg since 2013. Leading bush walks and experiencing this park on foot is a privilege that is yet to feel like work for him!

Bennet de Klerk runs a guide training school, Motsumi Bush Courses, from his farm at Mooihoek in the western Magaliesburg of South Africa. He has been a professional guide for almost 25 years and during that time has amassed over 10,000 hours of walks in dangerous game areas. Since 1996 he has specialised in training and assessing nature guides – over 700 at the last count – many of who have reached the highest echelon of the profession in South Africa. A significant number have themselves become guide trainers.

Until recently Bennet held the rank of lieutenant-colonel in the South African National Defence Force's Reserve Force.

Patricia Goodwin hails from a Liverpool-Irish family but is now a Welsh-speaking resident of North Wales. After nurse training and a variety of nursing posts she worked in sales and marketing for a leading pharmaceutical company. Now she runs a highly successful aesthetics company and is a FGASA-registered trails guide.

Chris Green has had a lifelong interest in the African bush, which led to a career conducting safaris with a focus on bushcraft and traditional skills. He is the owner and head guide of Cashan Africa Tours and Safaris. Also he is an accomplished artisanal baker in his spare time.

Sharon Haussmann is the owner of Khaki Fever, an outdoor and sports clothing shop in Hoedspruit. She lives in the bush and as a result is extremely bushwise. She has a specialist knowledge of and almost obsessive interest in spotted hyaenas. At the time of writing she is chairperson to the Balule Private Nature Reserve.

Brett Horley is a FGASA Level 3 trails guide, specialist birding guide and teacher of wildlife photography who has been guiding throughout the African continent for the past 11 years. Based in South Africa, he is the owner and sole leader of Brett Horley Safaris, a private guiding company specialising in customised itineraries with pre-arranged transfers and lodge bookings. In this rôle he has led field trips to Tanzania, Kenya, Botswana and Zambia, as well as in the areas he knows so well in South Africa, Timbavati and Klaserie.

Peter van Houdt is a lead trails guide and owner of Ubuntu Trails, offering walking safaris, leadership training, expeditions and private tailor-made safaris based on Ubuntu principles in pristine wilderness in Angola, Botswana, Mozambique and South Africa.

Phil Jeffery is an avid bush-person, having lived his life in Zambia. His early years were spent in the Luangwa Valley. But his heart belongs to the Kafue National Park where he has guided for the last 15 years and, together with a good friend, established Jeffery & McKeith Safaris and Musekese Conservation. He is a keen amateur photographer, private pilot and rugby fanatic.

Sophia Lehr hails from Cape Town, where she studied and obtained a Bachelor's in nature conservation. Then she followed her passion and became a field guide in Sabi Sands before moving into a career in management of bush camps and lodges. She still leads walking trails whenever possible.

Eugene Le Roux is a highly experienced field guide in South Africa who has completed several thousand hours on foot in the bush. Currently he is head guide at Kwa Maritane Bush Lodge in Pilanesberg National Park.

Calum McFarlane and his wife Sophie own and manage Lewa House, a safari camp in the Lewa Conservation Area of Kenya. Calum is also a lead walking guide there.

Shaun Malan is a professional guide and photographer with a number of publications in that field. He has guided in South Africa, Tanzania and Botswana, and presently works as a photographic guide for Machaba Safaris. His wife Elcke, who also features in this book, manages Machaba Camp on the Khwai river in Botswana.

Sam Mopalo is a guide working in Botswana. He was brought up in a family of guides, including his father and several uncles. He owns his own mobile safari company, Early Kingfisher Safaris.

Kane Motswana is the owner of Safari Embassy. He is one of the most renowned and highly sought-after guides and trackers in Africa, now with an international reputation following his highly successful starring appearance in the television film series 'Walking with Elephants'. The son of a San Bushman, he grew up in a remote village in northern Botswana, and carries with him a vast depth of knowledge passed down from his father and generations of bushmen before him.

Douglas Nagi is a gold-standard guide of the Kenya Professional Safari Guides Association (KPSGA) and currently works at Cottar's Camp in the Maasai Mara.

Mel Owtram is a field guide who, with her guide husband Ian, owns and operates a self-catering or catered bush camp, Antares, in the Greater Kruger with its Big Five. English by birth, Mel studied environmental biology at university before moving to South Africa to work on a game reserve where she met her guide husband Ian.

Brent Reed is a FGASA registered trails guide and assessor as well as co-founder of Okavango Guiding School and the mobile safari company, Letaka Safaris.

Rod Tether was born in Uganda, guiding since the age of 17 and now recognised as one of Africa's leading safari guides. His spiritual home remains Zambia's North Luangwa, where he and his wife Guz created and ran the fabulous Kutandala Camp for more than a decade before their children necessitated a move to 'civilisation'. Since then he's been leading mobile safaris to far-flung wild parts of Africa.

Themba Zwane is a tracker and guide at a lodge in the Greater Kruger National Park.

Polite Zwelile is a tracker at a lodge in the Greater Kruger National Park.

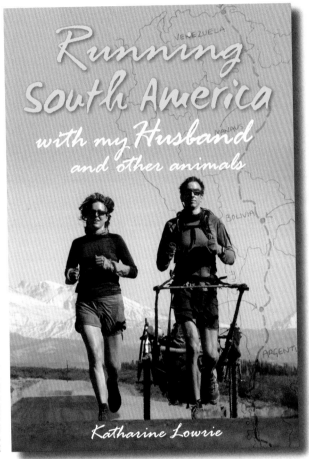

978-184995-362-7 £19.99

*It is a thrilling account punctuated by bizarre encounters
with incredible native wildlife...* Daily Express

Running South America *is an enthralling book
and without doubt one of the best I have read.*
Wildlife Detective, The blog of Alan Stewart

*This really is an inspiring book ...a lovely book which
will have you flinging off your shoes and embracing life.*
Burnley Express, Rebecca Hay

Whittles Publishing, Dunbeath, Caithness, Scotland, KW6 6EG
Tel: 01593 731333; *info@whittlespublishing.com; www.whittlespublishing.com*

Huw Kingston

MEDITERRANEAN

A year around a charmed and troubled sea

17 countries and 13 000 km
by kayak, foot, rowboat and bike

978-184995-274-3   £19.99

...an eye-opening journey around some extraordinary land and seascapes... a fascinating read for anyone with an interest in travel and Mediterranean culture. Lifeboat RNLI

If you're looking for a great read then you can't go past Mediterranean... an inspiring and entertaining read for all armchair adventurers. Great Walks Magazine

An entertaining page-turner that should not be missed. Sea Breezes

...this is a must read. Outer Edge

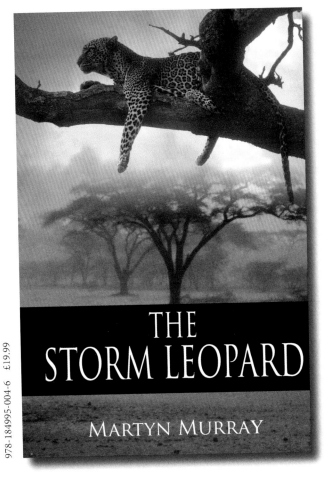

£19.99

978-184995-004-6

THE
STORM LEOPARD

MARTYN MURRAY

*This book comes highly recommended to anyone interested
in Africa's wild places and their continued protection. …
and a damn good read as well.* Environment

*…there is something in this book for everyone and it should
evoke a response… it will appeal most to the generalist
reader, especially those new to conservation biology.*
Bulletin of the British Ecological Society

The Storm Leopard *is an enthralling book. Martyn Murray journeys
from the Cape of South Africa to the Serengeti Plains, sampling
the mundane and especially the extreme places, and immersing the
reader in the richness of Africa. … [he] captures the vibes of Africa,
its customs and its moods.* The Storm Leopard *is a sheer joy to read.
Congratulations to the publishers Whittles for discovering Martyn
Murray – this is nature writing at its finest.* ECOS